Time to start
your own Reading.

All my Best.

2005

Cultivating A Winner From Within

8 Steps to Start a Revolution

Steve Walrath

Also the author of

Uncommon Sense for Unreasonable Times:
How to Live a Life That Matters

and

A Divorced Parent's Guide to Seeing Your Kids:
What judges, attorneys and your ex have not told you

Copyright © 2004 by Steve Walrath

ISBN 0-7414-1891-6

Published by:
INFI∞ITY
PUBLISHING.COM
519 West Lancaster Avenue
Haverford, PA 19041-1413
Info@buybooksontheweb.com
www.buybooksontheweb.com
Toll-free (877) BUY BOOK
Local Phone (610) 520-2500
Fax (610) 519-0261

Printed in the United States of America

Printed on Recycled Paper

Published December 2003

**Dedicated to
everyone who wishes
to make
a
difference**

Acknowledgments

Mike Duffy. Thank you for your help as a research assistant, chef extrordinaire, resident photographer and primary friend. A better brother could never be found.

Kathy Stevens. Your tireless efforts to edit, proof and prepare this book are driven from a deeper place to help others succeed. Your work is appreciated, valued and will impact generations to follow.

The staff of Great Radio Broadcasting and Great Ideas Company. Our personal and professional revolutions were intertwined with once-in-a-lifetime experiences and memories. Thank you for the passion, commitment and contributions from each of you.

My clients and friends around the world who have inspired me with their persistent hope and desire to seek a better way. Without your courage, advances would never be attained. Stay strong, stay true to your hearts.

My children Donny, Trevor and Stacy. With this book, I wish to pass on tools and skills that will assist you in making your own revolution of positive change. You, too, have inspired me with your inner strength and resolve that I could only hope to match. I love you with all my heart.

My Crime Stopper friends, here and abroad. A revolution has begun that we have the opportunity to magnify a hundred times over, making our communities a safer place to live and work. Thank you for your time, talents and generous hearts.

"The powerful play goes on,
and you may contribute a verse.

What will your verse be?"

Table of Contents

Introduction 1

Step 1: Set Your Foundation 15

Step 2: Establish Your Goal 33

Step 3: Build A Coalition 45

Step 4: Manage The Change 71

Step 5: Increase Commitment 83

Step 6: Stay Focused and Organized 107

Step 7: Pass the Baton 133

Step 8: Celebrate and Unite 149

Summary 165

Appendix: Analytic Outline 167

                       Lost at Sea Answers 173

                       Mantra Creation Worksheet 175

Notes 177

Workshops Available from The Center for Customer Focus . 179

About the Author 181

Introduction

Five minutes into my presentation on Dynamics of Customer Focus, a hand shoots up from the back of the room. The conference room is at what was formerly known as Comisky Field, home of the Chicago White Sox. It's crowded, packed full, shoulder-to-shoulder with employees from a local manufacturing company sent here for me to teach them how to better take care of the customer. The owner of the company is not present, nor was he present at the first of these workshops for his employees a month ago. I am introducing the subject of the day, the reason we are here and why they are sitting on hard metal chairs around tables formed in a giant U: the more we do our jobs from the customers' point of view, the more likely they are to buy from us and remain our loyal customers.

It makes sense.

Except to the guy in the back with his hand in the air. He usually sits in the back, chair tipped on two legs with his arms either crossed defiantly across his chest or lazily clasped on top of his head, a bored expression on his face, revealing he really has better things to do, like wash his car. Yet, he wishes to be heard, especially when the boss is not around.

I've been watching this one since I first walked in the room. Moses was how he introduced himself--a prophetic name, an ironic name in this instance, that I could not have made up on my own (I also had employees introduce themselves today as Elijah and Capt. Kirk, but I'm not sure, yet, how they will fit in to this scenario). His cap was on backwards. He hadn't shaved in two days and his ponytail hung limply down the middle of his back.

"This one is going to be a trouble," I begrudgingly thought to myself rather than thinking about the subject of the upcoming seminar. I can most always spot the malcontent, the one in the room who never wants to go along, always giving his buddy next to him a poke in the ribs, asking inane questions that don't pertain to the topic of the day such as, "When are we taking a break?" and "Can I step out for a smoke?" They always have to go to the bathroom, cough the loudest and give more smirks and whispers than a second grade reading room.

Moses was no different. Buckle your seatbelt. Here we go. He began with:

>*"You're just wasting your breath."*

>>*"We've been through all this before."*

>>>*"Nothing is ever going to change around here."*

And he didn't let up all morning.

Most every company I work with, teaching or giving a seminar, has several employees who will approach me, like spies in some dark secluded parking garage, their eyes twitching furtively from side-to-side, desperate not to get caught, and in varying forms and phrasing voice these same sentiments.

>*"Management will never change."*

>>*"They never let us give our opinion on anything."*

>*"They decide something and just drop it on us."*

>>*"We need training, but all they do is hand us a new piece of equipment and say 'figure it out.' By the way, we're going to start using it next week."*

"No one ever listens to us."

"This all sounds good, but the bosses will never go for it, so it really doesn't matter anyway."

I hear the same version from the manager's point of view, only it goes like this:

"Employees don't care. They just want a paycheck."

"I wish my people would support my decisions. It's for their own good."

"Things aren't as simple as they think. It's complicated."

"Why can't they just keep quiet and do their work."

"Employees today just don't care. Why can't they be more committed to doing a better job? That's how they'll get a raise."

At a company based in Seattle, I once gave my best effort at getting a group of employees to open up and talk, but they remained steadfast in their quiet and subdued responses. After three hours of cajoling them into reluctant participation, I stopped right in the middle of the workshop, actually right in the middle of a sentence, and said, "Okay, what's going on here?"

Their heads snapped simultaneously to the front of the room and looked at me as if I had just landed from Mars, eyes wide, mouths gaped open. Now that I had their attention, I pressed on.

"Look, I do this for a living and I can tell something is terribly wrong here. You haven't talked to each other once today. You seem not to care, yet I know you're good people. What is it?"

Silence weighed heavy as they looked at each other around the room. Eyeball met eyeball. Stare met stare as if with one word, the commandant would burst in and drag the verbal offender away to be tortured and never seen again. In the future, they would respectfully whisper his name around the water cooler and home campfires as an example of what happens when you dare to speak up.

Finally, one brave soul glanced up and timidly raised his hand, taking a risk that the others could only dream about. The others looked at him with varying expressions of, "What courage. What gumption. What a stupid guy."

"Do you see any management here? No. Do you know why? Because they sent us here to fix us. Nothing we say or do will ever change anything. So it just doesn't matter."

My heart broke with his words. These were good people. What little they did say indicated they were thoughtful and caring about their jobs, but over time had been sucked into a black hole of complacency and despair.

"It just doesn't matter."

That one statement sums up the same thoughts expressed to me by hundreds of employees and managers alike as I give seminars meant to pump them up, get them motivated, and presumably work more productively. Instead, too often I get,

"It just doesn't matter."

It cuts to the core of why so many working in our companies have given up, going through the day on autopilot, punching out as the sun sets and moaning, "Give me my check. I'm going home." A survey of American workers asked, "How many of you do not put any more effort into your job than is required to hold on to it?"

Answer - 50%

Another question, "How many of you are not working to your full potential?"

Answer - 75%

"It just doesn't matter."

So many working today feel anxiety about job security with layoffs, downsizing (right-sizing as it's now termed) and businesses going out of business. "Are we next?" We have an increasing sense of helplessness and anger, even feelings of guilt, knowing we could do more, should do more, but have no apparent reason. We are feeling more and more disconnected from the human beings around us, at work, home and in our communities.

We work and work, yet, too often, the perception turns into fact that it doesn't matter what we say or think or care to contribute about how to make things better, more efficient, more profitable -- no one pays any attention and, certainly, no one does anything about it.

Nothing will ever change.

Have you ever felt this way? Have you ever felt like what you're doing doesn't really matter? No one wants to pitch in, take a stand, do something to make a difference?

We all have. You are not alone.

It's a very difficult existence in which to live and work. It's discouraging. We go home and kick the cat or yell at the kids. It's frustrating. Depressing. Our well-intentioned contributions go unnoticed and, worse than ignored, they are dismissed as irrelevant by the simple phrase, "You don't understand. It's not that simple."

If this describes just a fraction of how you feel, then now is the time to start a revolution. This book will give you the tools to make it happen. A personal and professional revolution that will truly make a difference in your life, the lives of your co-workers, your family and kids. There is no better time than right now -- today.

> **"Lots of people are accepting what everybody else tells them. There have to be people who try to look into the future and say, 'Okay, I know everyone is operating on these premises now. But we've got to go another way'."**

With these words, Rudolf Giuliani took over as mayor of New York City--at that time, a sess-pool of drugs, welfare and rampant crime. Tourists feared walking down Broadway, hookers and the homeless owned Times Square. Giuliani could have said, "It doesn't matter. Nothing will change." But instead he said, "We've got to go another way."

You may or may not wish to attempt this, yet, you feel you have no choice. You are either going to start a personal and professional revolution of positive change or slowly die brain-dead over the next 30 years. I don't want to see that happen. You have too much to give to your co-workers, your families and to yourself. There are future generations, even now, imploring you not to give up, but to find a way to make this positive change happen.

Back in Chicago, back at Comisky Park, in that stuffy, crowded conference room, this is how I answered Moses to his defiant pronouncement, "You're just wasting your breath."

"I'm not wasting my breath because YOU can make a difference in the exact same job that you're doing. TOMORROW can be better than TODAY if you take the skills I am about to teach you, practice them, learn them and teach them to your coworkers. If everyone in this room said I was wasting my breath, except one person who said he'd try, then I have not wasted exercising my lungs. One person with hope and skill and the desire to make a change for the better is more powerful than a hundred complacent people who don't give a damn. It's YOUR choice. Will it be YOU who makes the difference or YOU who will be left behind?"

The room went flat with a deafening silence. Moses was quiet, but his eyes were glued to mine. He didn't blink, balk or flinch at my challenge. He was ready. I could see it. He was ready to take my message to heart and start a revolution of positive change. What I didn't know was how ready he was. A mere 24 hours later, he sidled up to me at the beginning of class, a sly smirk turning up the corners of his mouth.

"I thought about what you said. I can already feel my attitude changing. I feel differently about my boss, about my work and myself. I'm looking forward to today." He took his seat in the back. Same backwards hat, same limp ponytail, but a new expression on his face -- serene intentness. His pen was out, workbook open, he was ready to learn how to start a revolution.

Moses was about to lead his people, one more time, through history.

The principles outlined in this book will give you the tools and skills necessary to start a revolution. By reading them, you are also giving the first sign you have the desire, the heart and passion to make it happen. You will need to practice these principles, one at a time. Make them a part of your day, your thinking, and the way you go about your daily tasks.

You can start a revolution, creating positive change, beginning with your own personal and professional habits and attitudes.

You can start a revolution within in your department as a shop worker, receptionist, shipping clerk--any position within your company.

You can start a revolution as a manager or supervisor, guiding the people you are responsible for into a better, more productive working environment.

You can start a revolution as CEO with your employees, your peers and your customers.

You can start a revolution as a teacher, a doctor, or foreman.

You can start a revolution with your kids, as a mom, dad or grandparent.

You can start a revolution within your church, as pastor or parishioner.

You can start a revolution in your volunteer board meetings.

You can start a revolution within your community agencies, profit or not-for-profit.

You can start a revolution without anyone's approval or permission.

You can start a revolution of positive change by cultivating a winner from within, beginning with yourself and extending outward through your circle of influence at work, family and neighborhood. Negative circumstances don't have to stop you. We could say, "I can't afford it. I don't have time. No one will listen to me." Or we can adhere to the words of Maya Angelou:

> **"I can be changed by what happens to me.
> I refuse to be reduced by it."**

Step 1: Set Your Foundation. Assemble the seven preparations necessary to optimize your potential success. Prepare your values, your strengths, your weaknesses, your modeling behaviors, your game plan and your design for personal renewal. Prepare how you will accept input from others in order to have the truest, most complete information possible to formulate the clearest path to your ideals.

Step 2: Establish Your Goal. What is it you wish to accomplish? You must start with the goal as a precursor to making daily decisions and clarifying objectives. Make your goals big and inspiring, and you'll see resources open before you. Conduct a dream session to expand your vision and marshal collective enthusiasm into single, critical force.

Step 3: Build A Coalition. When you choose the first person to join your revolution, be sure they support and desire to contribute to its success. You will learn the necessity of getting all points of view before making a decision and the benefits of scheduling regular time for information exchange. With your mantra firmly established, you will have a single thought to guide your team's direction and course.

Step 4: Manage the Change. Some will help your revolution; others will attempt to assuage your hopes of change. Learn to use the "River Method" of managing change while continuously SCANing your team's position. Address the issues if WIIFM by attending to the needs of others first; then apply the benefits of self-observation and correction to stay on track.

Step 5: Increase Commitment. Ownership never comes naturally; it is a cultivated asset. Commitment/ownership is created through a five-stage cycle that moves a prospect from being unaware of your activities and intentions to asking how they can be involved. Laggards and innovators will both be prospective members and are converted through the same three-step process of affiliation, acknowledgment and authority. You will learn how to gain greater cooperation by applying the four-step technique of how to get anyone to do anything.

Step 6: Stay Focused and Organized. Time is your most valuable asset, and you certainly don't want to waste it with meaningless rhetoric when dealing with internal conflict. From now on, you will apply the Five Rules to Resolution to gain greater interdepartmental cooperation. You will take charge of the three most common traps that steal your precious asset of time: procrastination, perfectionism and carelessness in setting priorities.

Step 7: Pass the Baton. This will never be a solitary revolution. It will involve others who will take it to an even higher level than you can achieve yourself. Accomplishing this will require you to demonstrate attributes of the most successful leaders, presented in Step 7 as "leadership quick keys." Teaching skills will be paramount to passing the baton of values, principles and ideals. The techniques you will read about will help you analyze the process of adult learning and make your teaching time the most effective possible.

Step 8: Celebrate and Unite. Your revolution isn't complete without creating Positive Emotional Memories to motivate your team to greater heights. Then, generously apply the secret word, the most powerful word to change the experience of those who have made your revolution possible.

Resources in the appendix will analytically move you step-by-step through the process in linear form for those who like to see how to accomplish your revolution in sequence.

We will move through each step in a systematic fashion so you can apply the principles immediately after reading them. Each chapter will end with a summary of Revolutionary Tactics needed to accomplish that specific principle.

I would encourage your first read to be straight through to the end, so you see the whole picture of what you are moving through and towards. Get a feel for the process and its component action steps. Once you have read the book through, highlighting or underlining those parts that are most relevant to what you can do RIGHT NOW, go back to chapter one and re-read the principle. Do that principle for the next week. Review your progress and then re-read chapter two. Do that principle for the next week, review your progress and continue on. Do this chapter by chapter and, at the end of eight weeks, you will be amazed at your own increased influence and power. You'll be surprised at how your credibility and stature has risen among those you are in contact with, including management. You'll be impressed with how things really CAN change if you apply the eight steps to start a revolution.

If you are a supervisor, manager, CEO or owner of a company, these principles will give you the road map to building an effective and productive team of people who WANT to be part of a positive revolution. I've seen, heard about, and have participated in team building seminars that, in the end, are superficial and ineffectual. They are based on "U-rah-rah" feel good techniques including half-hearted expressions that "everyone is a part of this family" and "everyone needs to be involved," when the truth is you don't really mean it, especially with those with whom you have no desire to associate.

After a month of trying a few of these techniques, half-hearted team meetings and handwritten posters extolling the virtue of "Everyone Counts," it goes back to an environment of not caring, not listening, uninvolved complacency. The problem is, every time you attempt some form of change and it's unsuccessful, it becomes that much harder when something real and meaningful comes along.

These principles will help you create commitment on the part of
those you are supervising. Applying these principles can transform
a company culture -- one person at a time. When first attempting
these principles, you may receive the same type of response as in the
past: "We've heard it before. Blah, blah, blah. Things will be back
to normal shortly."

That is when you need to be consistent and persistent. Keep this
book handy. Re-read the portions where you need encouragement.
Some will never believe you. But many will see that you are sincere,
will follow your example, and contribute their own talents and
influences to cultivating a winner from within.

Can you really make a difference? Can one individual show a better
way for others to follow?

> **"The *little* difference in your life
> can make *all* the difference in your life."**

Yes, you can. But it requires a positive change on your part. You
will think new thoughts and speak different words.

❖   You will say "Yes . . . and " rather than "Yes . . . but."

❖   You will say "What if . . ." rather than telling someone "Here
is what you need to do."

❖   You will say "What would it take to . . ." rather than "Don't
screw up again."

❖   You will give before you take.

❖   You will produce before you consume.

❖ You will **Revive**, no longer living just to **Survive**.

This won't happen overnight, but you will see results within days. Your personal and professional revolution will be like tending the branches of a new vineyard. In the first year, the grape harvest is only 20% of what the second and third year produce. That's a phenomenal increase of 80% and more in the years to come! But only if you tend to the branches today. If left to themselves, they will fall to the ground and rot.

No fruit.

No harvest.

This book will show you how to tend your vineyard, coax the grapes to grow and flourish, create something new and exciting, something you can be proud of and pass on. Produce something your kids can use and find beneficial in their own lives, and for your grandkids and generations to follow.

This is that revolution.

The positive change may be needed in your personal life. You need different results than what you've been getting. Make a change...this book will show you how.

Maybe it's your professional life, at your work. You're struggling to get your employees or co-workers involved and produce to their full potential. This book will show you how to increase commitment and involvement.

You may be a line worker, accountant, customer service representative, salesman or warehouseman. You have a desire to make a difference, but you don't know how. You don't have the title or position of authority, so how do you make changes, make

something happen . . .start a revolution to make things better? This
book will show you the way.

You might be leading a church or a board of directors for a volunteer
agency. How can you create and expect revolutionary change when
there isn't any obligation on their part to follow you? How can you
motivate people to give their all and raise the level of their
accomplishment? This book will guide you to the answers you need.

Your prayer will parallel the prayer of Jabez, an Old Testament
believer who cried to the God of Israel:

> *"Oh that you would bless me indeed and enlarge my
> territory. That your hand would be with me and that you
> would keep me from evil that I may not cause pain."*

This is your chance, possibly your one opportunity.

This is your time to cultivate a winner from within.

Take the first step.

Turn the page.

Start a revolution.

Step 1: Set Your Foundation

*"Life is like a game of poker.
Are you willing to bet on yourself?"*

Walking into the room, I choose my spot for the day and sit down at a long, brown, wooded table. Opening my briefcase, I take out a thermos of milk, a sandwich, a set of headphones, cassette tape player and tapes. The tapes were not music to wile away the hours; they were instructional tapes on building a sales team, successful people management and leadership for the new millennium. This was my office--the public library back research room. I was three months away from taking ownership of my first radio station. I was 26 years old and I needed help--desperately! I never had this much responsibility and I needed to prepare myself. Everyday I went to my "office." Everyday I listened to tapes, took copious notes and built my knowledge in areas where I was deficient.

Every revolution must have a beginning, and this one begins with you. We can do nothing for others until we have first prepared ourselves. Do you think you're ready to start a revolution? Probably not. No one is ever totally prepared. It's like having children--there's never the perfect time, but when it happens, you want to be ready.

There are important issues we need to spend some time thinking about if we are to lead and guide those who will follow us. More importantly, even if no one joins our revolution, we need to know what it is we stand for and why.

> "Losers live the classic style in the
>   neverland of 'someday I'll . . .'
> While winners live each day
>   not in the future,
>   not in the past,
> But where someday becomes now."

We tend to hope, however misguided, that our circumstances will change and we won't have to put the effort into making a change ourselves. Question: will your boss just disappear? No. Will that irritating co-worker leave you alone? Probably not. Will your kids suddenly think you are their genius hero and your spouse think you are a god or goddess sent from the heavens? Ummm, I doubt it. Can you or I really change anyone else?

Absolutely not. There will always be those who will live their lives in perpetual melancholy doom or pathetic, miserable victimhood, blaming their woes on everyone but themselves. These people will die ticked off! They will be lying in their casket with a scowl, snarling at anyone who dares to look at them.

If these people won't change and our circumstances won't change for us . . . then who has to change? We do! Our response to this world, its circumstances and its people will have to change if we are to really make something happen. The sooner you accept and realize this fact to be true, the sooner you can put your energies into more positive and productive responses rather than fighting the unbeatable foe. What we must do is look within ourselves and perform a good, deep cleaning.

Not like power washing your vehicle. The first time I used a power washer, I put the quarters in and a powerful blast of water surged out of the nozzle. I sprayed and sprayed my truck from top to bottom. It looked wonderful! Glistening and clean. I could, once again, be proud of my truck.

But wait. I get home, hop out and . . . what is all this dirt doing all over my recently power washed truck? There are sweeps of grime and dust. How can they still be there after all my power washing? What I didn't know at the time is the power wash had only performed a surface cleaning. Without any scrubbing or brushing, the dirt will continue to cling to the paint.

The same result happens when we rush to make a few surface alterations that take little effort and never get down to the important matters of life. We resolve to do better without any substantive reasoning as to why. We are determined to make a difference without any knowledge of how we should go about accomplishing it. All are noble intentions, yet, all will fail without preparation.

"When a fish swims in the ocean, there is no limit to the water,
no matter how far it swims.
When a bird flies in the sky, there is no limit to the air,
no matter how far it flies.
However, no fish or bird has ever left its element.
Know where you must be in order to live
the life you lead.

There are seven areas we need to prepare if we are to start and lead a revolution. Not every revolution has to include others. In fact, the most important revolution will be the one you begin within yourself. To be successful, you must prepare your values, your strengths and your weaknesses. You will also prepare what behaviors to model, your design to get input from others, your game plan, and formulate your blueprint for personal renewal.

Prepare Your Values

Your values: what do you consider to be important enough that it takes first place over everything else? What do you consider to be second and third? What are your personal priorities? I have a friend whose mother is ranked 5th in his life . . . and that's okay! You might ask, how can that be? As his own mother once asked during the course of a visit.

He said, "It's easy ma. God is first. My wife is second. My son is third. I need a job to maintain and support my wife and son, so my job is fourth. You are fifth. And that's the way it is." She never asked again!

What have you determined is so important in your life that nothing much else matters except those few vital principles? When you know what they are, your decisions of what to do or not do become very clear and quite simple. No further complications are needed.

When I first took ownership of WGEZ radio, my one and only goal, my one and only issue of priority and value, was not to fail. Nothing else mattered. I had something to prove, as my dad had called me the night before I left for my new job, saying, "I hate to have to tell you this, but I think you're going to fail. I think you make poor decisions."

Every hour of the first 12 months in business I asked myself, "What do I have to be doing right now so that I can be in business tomorrow?" With that value firmly entrenched in my head, my decisions of what I should and should not be doing at any given moment became crystal clear.

We tend to over-complicate issues to begin with. The teachings of Christ, as found in the Bible, all boil down to two very simple principles: love the Lord your God and love each other.

The end. All else comes from these two principles. Yet, we've done quite a job of complicating that, haven't we?

When it comes to your place of work, what do you value most that will guide your decisions of what to do or not to do. I call this your mantra (explained in detail in Step 3: Build Your Coalition). You must know your personal mantra, your personal values, if you are to help others with theirs.

Prepare Your Strengths

Preparing your strengths means to evaluate and assess what you do well in terms of talents, abilities and skills. There is nothing wrong with knowing what you do well, in fact, it's essential. Your talents and abilities will be the foundation of your initial activities and what you will build on for the future

Do you speak well? Are you comfortable with groups? Do you complete your tasks on time? Can you see when someone else needs a helping hand? Can you think through problems to a logical conclusion? Can you envision things others don't? Can you keep doing a task until it's done . . . see it through to the end?

These are all strengths you may possibly possess, and you will need to hone and tone them like any athlete will do with his muscles. Give your personal strengths a workout by practicing and extending yourself. Do more than you think you can. Expand your capacity. Athletes do this by working out, doing exercises and practicing their skills to see where improvement can be found. We must do the same.

Practice your skills each day. Go beyond where you've been before. For example, read about things beyond your department, know what's going on in the whole company. Then read what's going on in your industry, know what's going on in other parts of the country. Talk to people who know things you wish to learn. Ask them questions, pick their brain. Take away nuggets of knowledge that you can apply right away to your daily living. Take a class at a local college. It doesn't matter whether your goal is to finish your degree or just gain more expertise in your strength; take a class and expand your horizon.

When teaching my staff, I use the analogy of a quiver. A quiver is a basket of sorts you put your arrows in and sling across your back. We each begin life with a set of arrows. Some are ready for immediate use, others need to be sharpened. Take out your strongest arrows, and be sure the tips are firm and sharp with knowledge and skill.

Discard those arrows that only take up room and are a hindrance to your performance. These arrows are attitudes of self-defeat ("whatever I try probably won't work"), the arrow of victimhood ("someone else is to blame for my lot in life"), the arrow of scarcity ("there isn't enough for everyone, I need to hold on to what I've got"), the arrow of immaturity ("they must come to me, I won't go to them"), the arrow of arrogance ("I am better than them"). The arrow of reprisal ("it's all their fault"), the arrow of selfishness ("I won't share what I have"), the arrow of complacency ("if it didn't work before, don't try it again").

These arrows get mixed in with the strong, sharp arrows of love, patience, kindness, understanding, compassion, and hamper your abilities when you need to strike a target. Get rid of these dull, useless arrows, get them out of your life, and gather arrows that will help strengthen you and guide you to hitting your target. Expand your quiver of arrows so when the time comes, you'll have the proper arrow to draw and let fly straight and true to your target.

Prepare Your Weaknesses

We all have areas that trip us up, hold us back and stop us from accomplishing what we want to achieve. Don't spend too much time in these areas, only because these weaknesses will probably never get you to where you want to be. If your weakness  is dealing with numbers (my personal Achilles heal), then no matter how much you study and how much you desire to be good at figures, in all likelihood, you will not become proficient at them. Don't sweat it. We cannot be good at everything.

BUT, as in my case, I must be aware of this weakness and be honest about my deficiency with it, or I can get into trouble real fast. Knowing I'm weak with numbers, I have studied financial books and business financial practices and am aware of what I need to know and do to stay out of trouble. (Pay your bills on time or you'll incur penalties. Pay your taxes or big trouble comes fast, etc.) Most importantly, build a network of people and systems that will support and bolster your weakness. It'll never become your strength, but it won't hurt you while you concentrate on building what you do well. The best advice concerning this issue is:

Soar with your strengths....manage your weaknesses.

Prepare Your Modeling Behaviors

We've heard it before and it remains a timeless truism: never ask someone to do what you aren't prepared to do yourself. I saw a wonderful demonstration of this principle while flying home late one night from a speaking engagement. Prior to takeoff, I noticed a United Airlines pilot sitting across the aisle, reading a book. I have flown a great deal, and I know the routine of the flight preparations. Tray tables up, seats in their full and upright position, flight attendants shutting the overhead compartment doors, and now the safety demonstration. We are asked to put aside our reading materials, cease our conversations and watch the video. Here is the oxygen mask. Here is your seat belt. Here is the safety card found in the seat pocket in front of you. So forth and so on.

Just like every frequent flier, I've heard these announcements a million times, so I tend not to pay as much attention as I should. But, glancing across the aisle, I noticed something. When the safety video began, the pilot put down his book, took off his glasses, and watched the video with an intensity as if seeing it for the very first time. When it finished, he went back to his reading.

Didn't he know how to put an oxygen mask on? Didn't he know how to clasp his seat buckle and tighten the strap? Didn't he know where to find the safety card? Of course, he did. What he was demonstrating was real leadership. He was doing himself what he would expect others to do. He was modeling the behavior he hoped others would follow. He was showing us that no matter how often he has heard the information or how proficient he personally might be with these issues, this is how we should behave during the safety demonstration.

Motor mimicry is a proven way to influence the behavior of others, simply by modeling yourself what you wish to see in others. For example, if I hit my thumb with a hammer, most people watching will grimace; they'll mimic my emotional state. In the book *Emotional Contagion*, the authors take this one step further. Mimicry, they argue, is also one of the means by which we infect each other with our emotions. In other words, if I smile and you see me and smile in response, it's not just you imitating or empathizing with me. It may also be a way I can pass on my happiness to you. Emotion is contagious.

We normally think of the expression on one's face as the reflection of an inner state. I feel happy, so I smile. I feel sad, so I frown. Emotional contagion, though, suggests that if I can make you smile, I can make you happy as well. If I make your frown, I can make you sad. Emotion, in this sense, goes outside-in.

If we think about emotion this way -- as outside-in -- it is possible to understand how some people can have an enormous amount of influence over others.

We need to first model the behaviors in ourselves that we desire to see in others. Only then will there be credibility and trust, as those watching can actually see what it is we're trying to accomplish.

> *"Directly modeling behavior demonstrates that someone without authority to tell others what to do can take an initiative. Your attempt to influence others' behaviors by example will be most effective when colleagues notice it."*

Prepare to Accept Input from Others

We need everyone's perspective if we are to create the absolute best work we can do. The illustration of this is found in an artifact called an Armillary Sphere. Reprinted below is an excerpt from a chapter entitled, "On Knowing It All" from my book *Uncommon Sense for Unreasonable Times: How to live a life that matters*:

The Armillary Sphere was used in the 1600s by the brilliant university teachers, philosophers and clergy of that day to explain how the world operated. They taught, by their observation and the observations of their fellow scientists from the past 1000 years, that the earth was the center of the universe. They could clearly see this was true with their crude and rudimentary instruments. In fact, anyone could see, with even an untrained eye, that the sun rose and fell around us! The stars and galaxies and all other planetary beings revolved around us!

Anyone with half a brain knows and understands that what we see and personally experience is truly fact. Correct?

For over 300 years, the Armillary Sphere was used to teach that the earth was the center of our vast universe. Respected men of that day all believed it to be true. Greek poets and philosophers going back to Aristotle and Ptolmey asserted this truth about the cosmos. Why test them? Aristotle, after all, was the greatest teacher of all time, so what sane person would question him? The Armillary Sphere was the artistic expression of that indisputable fact. Should anyone refute these tried and true observations–beware, run and hide from them! Copernicus was put to death for suggesting another explanation for the world. Galileo was excommunicated from the church and put under house arrest for the last 10 years of his life for supporting the notion that maybe it was us who did the revolving and not the sun.

There is only one problem with the Armillary Sphere. For all its beauty and artistic bends and curves of wood, bronze and iron, valiantly trying to fulfill what it was designed to explain–IT'S WRONG! Men of reputation and respect were wrong. Did they intend to be wrong? No, they were sincere. Were their observations fabricated? No, just incomplete. Did they mislead the ignorant masses they taught to believe something that wasn't completely true? Somewhat, but not with vile intent. It's just that they believed and formed their opinions only on what they could see *at that time.* Had they been given the opportunity to use the magnificent telescopes and satellites of today–or go so far as to travel into space–they would have formed a more accurate and complete understanding of how the universe actually worked. They just didn't have the tools. They went as far as they could using the limited technological and scientific talent of the time.

The practice, however, of squashing and dismissing any opinion different than our own continued. Let's not forget the witch hunts of early Colonial life where one was proven to be a witch through careful, personal observation. By the understanding of the "experts" of that day, if a suspected witch was thrown into a lake and floated, then she must be made of wood. Wood burns and so do witches, therefore, she must be a witch and immediately disposed of, usually, ironically, by burning her at the stake. Unfortunately, through this same test, one was proven not guilty of this atrocity by sinking into the water and drowning. Since rocks do not float and you did not float, you must be a rock and, therefore, not a witch! Congratulations on securing your innocence and salvaging your immortal reputation!

It's surprising what people will do for what they believe to be true.

Rightly AND Wrongly.

I was looking for an Armillary Sphere of my own and was given one by a friend at Christmas. I have it sitting on my library table and see it many times during the day. For all its beauty and historical significance, it means only one thing to me. It is my daily reminder that as smart as I think I am, as much as I think I know the truth by my own observation and experience, I don't know everything I THINK I know.

Steven Covey writes, "Almost every significant breakthrough is the result of a courageous break with traditional ways of thinking."

I will never have the complete picture with just my own observation. I cannot base my response on only what I see or hear during a specific time. I may not have the right tools to discern and understand the whole picture. I may not have a clue as to why someone may act the way he does until I explore further. I have to see things from a different view, an alternative perspective from my own. I may have to climb a ladder or ride in a spaceship to get the proper view–to find out what is true. But how often do I take the opinions of others, even people I highly respect, rather than find out for myself? How often do I base my opinion on such limited information without going to the heart of the matter? They, too, are only working from a limited view. Could they be wrong? For all their genius and love of truth, might they be teaching me something that isn't exactly correct?

Everyone's view is skewed.
Everyone's perspective is shaded.
No one knows it all.

> *From the cowardice that is afraid of new truth,*
> *from the laziness that is content with half-truth,*
> *ffom the arrogance*
> *that thinks it has all truth,*
> *O God of Truth deliver us."*

Prepare Your GAME Plan

Using the acronym GAME is a great way to plan your revolution. When you say you have your "game" on, you know if you are prepared to actually get something done or if you're just wishing upon a star. Don't wish your life away . . . get your game on and make something happen.

G stands for goal. Establish your goal. What is it you wish to see changed? Without your goal, you will have nothing to shoot for, and you'll never know if you've made it. Your goal becomes the clear and concise guide that you can remember and steers you to make correct daily decisions. (I will delve deeper into this subject in Step Two: Establish Your Goal.) Know Your Goal First!

A stands for action. What physical action steps will be needed to accomplish your goal? Notice I said PHYSICAL action steps. Did I say, get a better attitude? Did I say change your personality or, worse, attempt to change the personality of others? No. Actions are not connected to feelings. Physical action steps are those things you are going to do whether you feel like it or not. What physical action steps will be needed to accomplish your goal?

M stands for measurement. What measurement tools will you need to chart your progress? Without measurement tools, you won't know if you are really moving ahead. You might use your measurement tool once a day, once a week or once a month; frequency isn't the primary issue. Your measurement tool will be your guide to maintaining your course of direction or adjusting your methods and activity, depending on your progress and heading.

E stands for Evaluation. How will you know if your measurements are accurately marking your progress? Are your action steps leading you toward the goal you wish to achieve? Has the goal changed during the course of your implementation? Every step is in flux until you reach your destination. These answers are found only by continuously evaluating your current position in comparison to where you wish to be. Never stop evaluating. It's the only way we learn.

Do you have your game on? Prepare for your revolution by putting your game on and really make it happen.

Prepare Your Blueprint for Personal Renewal

 You will get tired. You will get worn out and discouraged. Sometimes it seems you will work and work and make very little progress. Athletes get tired. And when they do, they rest. Plan for personal renewal times, times to back off and renew your strength and objectives. When I've been on the road for an extended time, I get home and rest. I might take a WHOLE DAY and do NOTHING. I'll read a bit or watch movies or go for a ride on the motorcycle. But I literally accomplish nothing . . . on purpose! This is renewal time. A time to rest and relax and let my intellectual and physical muscles heal and restore.

Your car needs gas. You don't drive it until it runs empty (hopefully!). When you see your gas gauge running low, you STOP! You stop at a gas pump and refill the tank. Plan to STOP on a regular basis to take in new fuel and refreshment. Get proper sleep and food-- fuel for energy. Then when you re-enter your revolution, you will have the energy you need to carry you to the next level.

In many respects, personal renewal means assessing your previous six preparations. Are they intact? Do any need re-adjusting or fine tuning? Sometimes, we just need to dejunk our lives in order to keep our inner self clean, pure and available. Wayne W. Dyer has a wonderful eight point plan for dejunking your inner self:

➡ *People are often unreasonable, illogical, and self-centered. Forgive them anyway.*

➡ *If you are kind, people may accuse you of being selfish, with ulterior motives. Be kind anyway.*

➡ *If you are successful, you will win some false friends and some true enemies. Succeed anyway.*

➡ *If you are honest and frank, people may cheat you. Be honest and frank anyway.*

➡ *What you spend years building, someone may destroy overnight. Build anyway.*

➡ *If you find serenity and happiness, people may be jealous. Be happy anyway.*

➡ *The good you do today, people will often forget tomorrow. Do good anyway.*

➡ *Give the world the best you have, and it may never be enough. Give the world the best you've got anyway.*

In many respects, you never stop preparing yourself. You are always finding new interests, new ways in which to use your talents, new avenues you never expected or thought of taking when you began. When I first wrote *A Divorced Parents Guide To Seeing Your Kids; what judges, attorneys and your ex have not told you*, I never thought of becoming certified as a mediator in family court. But the more I shared my experiences and insights to help parents see and maintain a strong relationship with their kids, the more I felt that I might make a difference right in the court system itself. So I took classes and read books and talked with attorneys and other mediators. I prepared myself by expanding my skills and stretching my personal horizons.

So will you.

Never stop preparing. Never stop learning. Never stop moving ahead in positive directions. This will be the groundwork for the success of your personal and professional revolution.

Now, set your foundation.

Revolutionary Tactics To Set Your Foundation

➡ Our circumstances will not change for us. To attain a more fulfilling future, WE must be the ones to change.

➡ Perform a deep cleaning of your life through the technique of PREPARATION.

➡ Prepare what your values will be; what is important to you? Stay firmly focused on these values, as they will guide your daily choices.

➡ Prepare your strengths; what do you do well? Practice your skills and expand your capacity for even greater success.

➡ Prepare your weaknesses; what do you need help with? Surround yourself with a system and network to support what you don't do as well as others.

➡ Prepare your modeling behaviors; what will others see you doing? One of the most powerful ways to influence people is by their seeing from you, exactly what is expected of them.

➡ Prepare to accept input from others; are you willing to listen to a different point of view? The Armillary Sphere teaches us to solicit all perspectives if we are to really know the truth of what is best.

➡ Prepare your blueprint for personal renewal; do you need a rest? In the midst of your revolution, you need to refresh and re-energize your physical, intellectual, social and spiritual batteries. Make a plan for consistent renewal for optimum performance.

STEP 2 **Establish Your Goal**
STEP 1 Set Your Foundation

Step 2: Establish Your Goal

"Direct your life with purposeful choices, not with speed and efficiency. The best musician is one who plays with expression and meaning, not the one who finishes first."

It's a glorious, sunny morning. You decide to invite a number of close friends to enjoy this resplendent day by cruising the bright, blue ocean on your very own yacht. (Stay with me. This is my vision of your life!) It was only meant to be a three-hour cruise (hopefully you packed enough coconuts to last three television seasons on a deserted island. If you don't know what I'm talking about, watch reruns of Gilligans' Island!) A storm arises out of nowhere. (Thankfully, not the "perfect" storm. Watch the movie! Are you still with me?)

Your yacht sinks and all that remains is you, your friends, a rubber raft, a book of matches and three, one dollar bills. You have limited space in the raft with room for only a few essential items. From the following list, what would you keep first, second, third, etc.?

Sextant
Shaving Mirror
Five-gallon can of water
Mosquito netting
One case of Army C rations

Maps of the Pacific Ocean
Seat cushion (flotation device)
Two-gallon can of oil-gas mixture
Small transistor radio
Shark repellant
Twenty square feet of opaque plastic
One quart of 160-proof Puerto Rican rum
Fifteen feet of nylon rope
Two boxes of chocolate bars
Fishing Kit

When I present this exercise to my organizational workshops, most groups will immediately begin discussing the advantages and disadvantages of each item, assessing their individual value in the quest for a solution to the puzzle. The water is needed, but are the maps of the ocean? Do we keep plastic for catching rain or a seat cushion as an emergency flotation device. Would you keep the chocolate over the fishing kit? Or vice versa? Do you even know what a sextant is or what it can do?

The problem is, most groups NEVER establish their goal before discussing and deciding what is most important to keep! They leap right in, a sudden and feverish buzz filling the room as opinions, experiences and far-fetched memories of camping criss-cross back and forth. What goes unsaid in this frantic exercise is . . . it doesn't matter what you keep if you don't know your goal. And there are a number of goals that could be established in these circumstances.

☆   If you goal is short-term survival, you keep the water, Army C rations and chocolate at the top of your list.

☆   If your goal is long-term survival, you'd keep the water, Army C rations, fishing kit, plastic and maybe the rope.

☆   If your goal is to find land, you'd retain the maps of the Pacific Ocean, the sextant (if someone knows how to use one) and the seat cushion if you need to swim to shore.

☆   If your goal is to be rescued, you need the shaving mirror for signaling, the oil-gas mixture to light on fire for smoke and the can of water.

☆   If your goal is to go out with a party, you keep the rum first, the chocolate for fondu and the radio to dance your last hours away!

(The answers, according to the U.S. Merchant Marines, are found in the Resource Appendix: Lost At Sea. How do your answers compare with theirs?)

The lesson to understand is how important it is to establish your goal BEFORE you make any decisions about what it is you are going to do. Your survival may depend on knowing your goal and knowing you have the right goal. Most of us spend much of our time on our activities, mainly because the goal has not been firmly established. If you don't begin with the goal, it doesn't matter what you're doing! Always start with the goal.

It's doesn't help to climb a ladder really fast if it's leaning against the wrong wall!

You must start with the goal. What is the end result of the change you wish to initiate? You must be able to see it, feel it, know what it looks like, know what it looks like when its done. With your goal in mind, you can picture how people will interact with each other, respond to each other, listen and value each other. You see your respond to each other, listen and value each other. You see your accomplishments in action.

> **You hang a man NOT for stealing a horse --**
> **You hang a man to keep a horse from being stolen.**

Your goal comes first. Your decisions of what activities you ought to be doing will then become much clearer. Without the goal firmly set, you'll be running around, stirring people up, inflaming their hopes and fears, only to find yourself in a vicious circle, not knowing where you are going or whether the trip is even worth the hassle.

> **I have good news and bad news.**
> **The bad news is we're lost.**
> **The good news is we're making great time!**

Four Principles to Understand About Goals

① *Great goals attract great people.* When starting our companies, we use to say, "Do it big or don't get out of bed." Expand yourself. Winners set stretch goals, then work incrementally and relentlessly toward them. Set your goal to something you can't imagine possible today, then plan how to achieve it.

I posted the following statement on my bulletin board the first day I took over a losing radio station. It guided my efforts to reach higher than I thought possible and accomplish more than I could imagine.

What is not yet done
is only what we have not yet
attempted to do.

Great goals precede resources. Too often, we look further down the road than we should and say, "I don't see how this can happen. I can't speak in front of groups. I can't lead. I don't see who can help me." We look at what's missing and allow that to keep us from making great goals. Remember, resources do not show themselves when you haven't made up your mind what it is you want to do. Do it big or don't get out of bed!

Focusing on our great goals opens up resources. Take the first step toward your seemingly impossible goal, and you'll be amazed at what doors begin to open. Tell people you trust and who support you about your great goal and someone will say, "I know who can help you." Resources open AFTER you set your great goal. Robert Schueller once said,

> *"Money is never the issue. Money flows to ideas that have credibility and urgency."*

The idea, the great goal, always opens up resources.

Stop your great goals and the resources dry up. As soon as you begin to minimize the vision of what you wish to accomplish, the resources are no longer at your fingertips. Your mind begins to close, you no longer "see" what others tell you was not there to begin with. You believe the falsehood that you're just like them and you can't do any more.

Never stop establishing great goals. Small goals create the following characteristics in people:

* They too often become intimidated.
* They work alone rather than build a team of success stories in others.
* They don't like to leave their comfort zone.
* They feel inadequate in the presence of other successful people.
* They avoid the big idea, the big goal, for fear of rejection.
* They prefer to work with less successful people who are more easily led and less motivated.

Stop the great goals and the resources dry up. nstead, continually establish SMART goals.

S.M.A.R.T. Goals Succeed

Smart goals have the following characteristics. They are:

Specific: Your great goal needs to be specific, not general. In order to hit a target, you focus on just one thing, not the whole broad range of your surroundings. What specifically do you wish to accomplish? Better cooperation between co-workers? The opportunity to have more say in what goes on in your department? Be specific when describing the end result your desire.

Measurable: Your great goal needs to have a tool that will indicate whether you are making progress or not. Without measurement, you might not know if you've achieved it! A measurement tool might be the number of times something happens that is consistent with the results of your goal. It could be a measurement of increasing the quality of your interactions with other people. It could be a comparison of where you are today in relation to where you were a month ago or year ago. Measure it or lose it.

A **ction-orientated.** Fill your great goals with physical action steps. It takes physical action steps to achieve anything, something bodily you have to do. Don't set a goal of changing your attitude, or worse, the attitude of someone else! Attitudes and feelings follow the success of your physical action steps.

R **ealistic.** Your great goal IS achievable, and achievable by you. You may not see exactly how at this time, but you will do it. Saying you wish to be President might be noble, but not realistic. Or saying you wish to walk on the moon requires a bit more help from people in different fields of expertise. Don't set yourself up to fail with a goal that is impossibly unrealistic, yet, at the same time, reach higher and higher for your goals.

T **imely.** Your great goal needs a time element. Saying "you'll get around to it when you can" or "you'll take that first step as soon as possible" just won't cut it. Set a date, set a time. Your goals will never be accomplished if you wait for that "just right time."

To start a revolution, you will set your foundation by preparing yourself, but soon you'll have to expand your preparation to include the goals of others.   That requires getting their input and participation. I will spend considerable time explaining this in Step Five: Increase Commitment, but for the purpose of goal setting, I'll give you one of the more creative and enlightening exercises you can do when drawing the goals of others into your revolution. We called it a "dream session."

Dream Sessions

What do you do with an AM radio station that no one listens to and is losing $10,000 cash every month? The employees are discouraged.

There is no money for raises, barely enough to survive bill paying month-to-month. You have limited resources and slim prospects for a prosperous future. The answer for our company (and our revolution) was to hold a dream session.

The purpose of a dream session is to move everyone directly affected by your plans from a current state of complacency and narrow mindedness into a future of unlimited possibilities. Not an easy task. Yet, possible. The object is to create a safe environment where ideas are freely exchanged, nothing is out of the realm of discussion, and you have a smidgeon of fun in the process. You want people to think big, bigger than they ever have, bigger than they think even possible. Implement these four stages to creating a vigorous dream session.

Stage 1: Choose the proper location.

I believe you send a message when a brainstorming session is held off-site from where normal business is handled day-to-day. The message conveyed is, "this is <u>not</u> business as usual." I want my participants to immediately and completely be focused on the task at hand and not be distracted by phone calls to make, papers to produce, or normal conversations. The environment can be anywhere except where you normally meet. I've used the back room of a restaurant, a hotel conference room, an upper floor meeting room of supper club (where the owner also lived, so we had to walk past personal living spaces, including the sight of wet socks hanging over a curtain rod, and articles of clothing strewn about the floor . . . Just keep looking straight ahead. I don't want to know!) I've held these meetings in my own living room at home. The location must be outside the norm and at a neutral site. Include snack food and beverages. I don't know what it is about food that relaxes a group of people, but the social and creative production is increased ten-fold with food and drink.

The room should have a blank pad on an easel with clean, bold, new markers. Have masking tape handy for hanging the ideas on the wall when a page is full. I would suggest this rather than a wipe board or chalk board, because you want to keep the fresh, exciting ideas in front of the group to keep their thoughts stimulated and engaged.

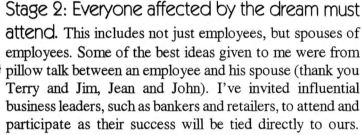

Stage 2: Everyone affected by the dream must attend.
This includes not just employees, but spouses of employees. Some of the best ideas given to me were from pillow talk between an employee and his spouse (thank you Terry and Jim, Jean and John). I've invited influential business leaders, such as bankers and retailers, to attend and participate as their success will be tied directly to ours. They all have a stake in the outcome, and some of the best ideas originate from outside eyes, fresh and unencumbered by bias or familiarity.

Stage 3: Follow the Rule
There is only one rule for a dream session idea; the rest are guidelines for any normal brainstorming session. The rule is:

> **Any idea generated cannot be hampered for lack of money, time or people.**

Most ideas are stamped as "undoable" because there is never enough money (not in the budget), never enough time (I can't get everything done as it is), and never enough manpower (we're stretched too thin already). Take away money, time and people and the mind travels to places it's never been before. The possibilities are endless. The potential for success is closer than ever.

Once this rule is presented, then let the ideas flow. Write <u>every</u> idea on the pad. There are none too far-fetched or ridiculous (someone will always say they'd like the company to provide a new car every year or a yearly 20% raise). Write it down. I want them to say, "why not?" rather than, "that'll never happen." What would they like to see accomplished in the next five years? What personal interests would they like to see fulfilled? Take away every obstacle, roadblock and hindrance. NOW, what would you like to do?

Stage 4: Prioritize the Ideas

Once you have filled two, three or four pages of ideas and posted them on the wall, begin an initial group prioritization. With a red marker, circle three ideas that, as a group, you would like to see completed in the next year. Now ask, out of these three ideas, which one idea would they most like to see completed?

Take that idea and write it across the top of its own, clean page. Underneath that idea, list the objectives that need to be met in order for the idea to become a reality within the next year. Below each objective, identify the tasks that are necessary for completing the objectives that fulfill the idea.

Once you have completed stage 4, then celebrate the contribution of the group. Congratulate them on thinking big, wanting to accomplish great things and end the session. The dream session is not meant to be a planning meeting, but rather a creative session of free thinking about an exciting and more inspiring future. The reason you take one idea and follow through with the initial planning is to enlist volunteer support and create accountability between each person who has a task in the process.

The ideas created can then be used as stepping stones for future planning meetings and goal setting.

What is most important after this dream session is for everyone to visibly see, within a very short amount of time--a few days or a week at most--that something is being done. The worst thing that can happen is no one sees any activity pertaining to the objectives and ideas presented. They will never open up again with the same passion and involvement as once exhibited.

One company had an idea generated from the warehouse crew. The warehouse workers said there was a leak in the back corner of storage right over the pallets that were loaded and ready for shipping to the customer. The product they produce is packaged in cardboard cases. When the water dribbles on the cases, the cardboard becomes wet and slimy and eventually falls apart. The warehouse crew simply asked, can the leak get fixed so our customer is not receiving wet cardboard cartons?

When the management team and I were discussing the ideas generated in our session, they asked me what idea I thought should be considered first? My answer was simple: FIX THE LEAK! They've been dealing with this issue for years. Fixing the leak would show everyone this dream session had meaning, and something positive will be generated from actually doing the follow-up tasks. A maxim of marketing is:

> **Say what you're going to say – say it – then tell them what you've said.**

The same is true with goal setting.
* Tell everyone what you're going to do.
* Do it.
* Then tell them what you've done.
* And then tell them what's coming up next.

Nothing you plan, nothing you do, no activity or frantic hustle and bustle will ever be successful unless you first establish the goal.

It all beings with the goal.
Start with the goal.

...onary Tactics to Establish Your Goal

➡ Understand that Great Goals will attract Great People. Think big or don't get out of bed. Be ready to recognize that "star" individual who can take you to the next level of success. Invite him to join your revolution.

➡ Great Goals Precede Resources. You must begin with your goal first. Don't look too far down the road, or the impossibilities of your goal will override your passionate commitment. Rather, establish the great goal, then prepare yourself for opportunities to unfold.

➡ Focus on your great goal, then resources open up. Ask people to help or direct you to the next step towards fulfillment of your goal. Others will step forward when they know what you are trying to accomplish and offer assistance. Accept their help with sincere appreciation and gratitude

➡ Stop your great goal and the resources dry up. The smaller your goal, the lower your expectations become. Soon, the doors will close, the avenues of opportunity are shut down. Keep your goals in ever-increasing spheres of greatness, and you will never lack for resources to fulfill them.

➡ Evaluate your goals to assure they are SMART: specific, measurable, action-oriented, realistic and timely.

➡ Expand your vision with a group dream session. Take away the hindrances of money, time and people, and let the ideas flow.

➡ Prioritize your ideas to one you'd like to complete this year. Begin to publicly work on it within days to demonstrate your commitment to its fulfillment. Then others will volunteer to help, as well.

Step 3: Build A Coalition

"We have all encountered people who seem barely awake, who squander their lives, who blind themselves to what is taking place within and around them, who do not care about what they do, how they do it, to whom or why. This is the atrophication of life."

Consider the following puzzle. If I gave you a single sheet of paper and asked you to fold it over once, and then take that folded paper and fold it over again, and then again and again until you have folded the original paper 50 times, how tall do you think the final stack would be? Imagining in our mind's eye, we envision something the size of a large telephone book.

The real answer is the height of the stack would approximate the distance to the sun. And if you folded it one more time, the stack would be as high as the distance to the sun and back. This is an example of what, in mathematics, is called a geometric progression. Revolutions are another example of a geometric progression; when it spreads, it doubles and doubles until it has grown from, in our example, a single sheet of paper, all the way to the sun in fifty steps.

We have a hard time imagining this kind of progression, because the end result seems far out of proportion to the cause.

With a revolution, we need to prepare ourselves for the possibility that sometimes big changes follow small events, and sometimes these changes can happen very quickly. But they are all based on the premise that we cannot do it alone. Any revolution requires the input, participation and involvement of like-minded individuals. Yet, it will begin with one.

The American revolution did not begin with a mass of citizens taking up arms and engaging battle with Britain. Its roots began with a single individual recognizing a need and doing his part to make a change for the better. One person doing something will always accomplish more than many doing nothing. But, are you aware of a man named William Dawes, a tanner who lived in proximity to Paul Revere and actually rode from town to town that historic night, as did Paul, to spread the word of the coming British invasion?

Why do we remember one man and not the other? They had the same information. They used the same method of communication. They even rode the same mode of transportation. Why was the message of one heeded while the other was ignored? In fact, so few men from one of the towns Dawes rode through fought the following day that some historians concluded it must have been a strongly pro-British community. It wasn't. he people of this community just didn't find out the British were coming until it was too late. If the revolutionary message itself was all that mattered, Dawes would now be as famous as Paul Revere. He isn't.

The answer lies in the people we choose to enlist in our revolution. The coalition of individuals that form the core of our reformation will carry the significance of whether the message is conferred from person to person, department to department, or whether it is lost in the battle of complacency.

Many times it's not the content of your message, but who you share it with that will determine whether you achieve success or failure.

To start a revolution, you cannot do it alone. our vision and goal may take root in your individual conscience, but it will take many others to enact and make the changes you desire. To accomplish this, you must build a coalition, a group of like-minded individuals who envision the same goal and its potential for good. This coalition is built through the following four principles of actions and attitudes:

First: choose one other person to share your thoughts.
This person should be someone you trust, who has persuasion within his immediate sphere of influence and who is not jealous or intimidated by someone else's leadership. This person has to have a sincere heart, wanting others to succeed. Begin
by using words such as, "what if . . . " or "what would it take to. . ." when discussing a future goal. This allows you to present options for action without requiring a commitment, at this point, on their part. Through this technique, you can also gauge their response and receptiveness to your ideas. (See Step 7: Pass the Baton, for other quick keys to use during this phage.)

Once you see the light snap into their eyes and they begin to contribute their own points of view to create a combined future vision, then you know you have a beginning. Continue to talk with them about the objectives, and the reasoning for each objective, in its relation to the goal. Take notes on your discussions and incorporate as many of their ideas as your own into the process.

The key to successful leadership today is *influence*, not authority.

At this point, each of you choose two other people to join your team. You'll now have six people whom you are recruiting to ride your revolutionary train, which brings us to the next principle of thought and action.

*Second: elicit input from each individual. N*o one will ride your train for very long unless their input is valued and included. Seek out the thoughts of all people involved, stake-holders in the outcome, in order to increase their buy-in to the goals and ferret out any dissension before it festers and builds into a counter-force against you.

 Always **CBD**: **C**onsult **B**efore **D**eciding. It serves two purposes. It draws on a wider base of ideas and talent and tends to increase engagement and commitment from those consulted for their thoughts.

How do you achieve 100% participation and involvement? By following these thought and action patterns:

You are not the sole source of wisdom and ideas. In fact, if you don't get the input of others, you will be building an armillary sphere rather than a new and brighter future (review Step One; Prepare to accept input from others). This attitude, on your part, is essential -- others will pick up on your subconscious signals of superiority if that is how you really feel about them. Evaluate your personal goals and agenda to be certain you are not subverting your own good intentions. This is wonderfully illustrated by the following, unique picture.

Are there people you know who best represent the rope on the left? They are orderly, structured and follow a specific pattern of behavior. They tend to follow the rules, do not like surprises and question why we should attempt to "fix" something if it isn't broke.

Are there people you know who are represented by the rope on the right? They tend to be nonchalant, appear to be less concerned with protocol and more concerned with getting on to the next activity. Some may label them careless, while others would call them carefree.

There are strengths and weaknesses with each person represented by the ropes. Neither is totally right nor totally wrong. There is a lot of information missing with this picture pertaining to context and reasoning behind the way the ropes are tied. The primary lesson is that we need all points of view if we are to have the greatest level of success. Don't get caught up in personality traits at the expense of complete knowledge.

Specifically ask every individual, whether one-on-one or in a group, what their thoughts are and how they would make this goal better. Refrain from making statements during this process. You don't want to be **telling** them what they ought to be believing. You ask questions for the purpose of discovering what **they** are thinking and feeling.

In other words, do not ask leading questions or questions that actually reveal YOUR personal view point. Don't ask, "This is a good idea, isn't it?" "There isn't any reason we shouldn't go ahead with this, is there?" Instead ask, "What would you do with this goal to make it better?" "What did you think about this point? Is it a valid concern?"

Asking the following types of questions will elicit a higher level of response:

- Open ended questions (who, what, why, where, how,).

- Using the phrase, "what if. . ." in order to evoke a response and get their point of view on future activities.

- Ask alternative-of-choice questions such as, "If you were doing this, would you choose, A or B?" In terms of alternative preferences, only give two, no more than three choices. This way, they can process the evaluative information rather than becoming confused, resulting in no decision at all.

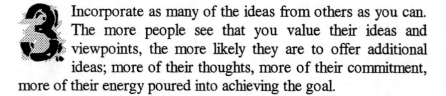 Incorporate as many of the ideas from others as you can. The more people see that you value their ideas and viewpoints, the more likely they are to offer additional ideas; more of their thoughts, more of their commitment, more of their energy poured into achieving the goal.

Johnny Carson was the master at embracing the comedy of others, a wildly unnatural act among comedians. As he once explained,

**"Never compete with them (your guests).
The better they are, the better the show is."**

Require involvement and contribution from each individual or excuse their attendance form your group. Hangers-on only drain the thought process with comments and dissension, without actually making a positive investment. They must contribute in a forward thinking, productive manner, or you must find ways to let them go about their life without hindering yours. There are some who sit through meetings, don't say a word, don't volunteer to help, or plead they are too busy to participate; yet, they sit there sucking up oxygen and space. They have adopted the "group" mentality assuming that *someone* will do what needs to be done.

This group mentality is characterized by the tragic story of the 1964 stabbing death of Kitty Genovese, a Queens, New York, resident who was chased by her assailant and attacked three times on the street as 38 of her neighbors watched from their windows. During this time, however, none of the 38 witnesses called the police. It was first assumed that apathy was the big-city culprit or indifference to one's neighbor as a conditioned reflex of life in New York. The truth, however, turns out to be a little more complicated.

Two New York City psychologists subsequently conducted a series of studies, trying to understand what they dubbed the "bystander problem." What they found was when people are in a group, responsibility for acting is diffused. They assume that someone else will make the call, or they assume that because no one else is acting, the apparent problem isn't really a problem at all.

Other studies have shown that in a tug-of-war contest, the combined power of everyone pulling is LESS than the sum of the pulling strength of each individual. Why? We don't give ALL our energies when we assume that someone else will pick up the slack.

This is the importance of requiring the participation of every individual, no matter how small or seemingly insignificant the offering.

THAT'S NOT MY JOB!

This is a story about four people named Everybody, Somebody, Anybody and Nobody. There was an important job to be done, and Everybody was sure that Somebody would do it. Anybody could have done it, but Nobody did it. Somebody got angry about that, because it was Everybody's job. Everybody thought Anybody could do it. It ended by that Everybody blamed Somebody when Nobody did what Anybody could have done. – Author Unknown

Don't let it happen to your revolutionary team.

Act and contribute, or don't be there.

> **"People do things they want to have meaning and are personally fulfilling. If you have a choice between capital intellectual property or really good people, I'd always choose the people."**

Third: Consistently schedule times to exchange information. This could be via a staff meeting, conference tele-call or a weekly chat. No matter the method or convention used, there must be time for the interactive process in order to move a goal forward. Notice, I specifically said there must be interactive time **"in order to . . ."**

This is the main problem with meetings. There is no purpose. There is no "in order to . . ." Test everything you do with "in order to . . ." Does the activity move the process forward toward achieving the goal? If not, don't do it.

> *"Do not take the next steps, no matter how simple, that fail to take you in the direction you want to go."*

To this end, here is the content of the perfect meeting. The meeting length is not the issue; more important is the substance:

Purpose: Have you formulated a list of goals to be accomplished during this meeting?

Thinking: Are we moving logically from symptoms through diagnosis to planning?

Learning: Are we moving quickly between preparation, action, and review?

Engagement: Does every task have someone responsible for it? Are we inviting and welcoming the ideas of all?

Feedback: Do we regularly offer appreciation and support? Do we exchange specific coaching for improvement?

Begin your meeting with a statement of purpose. Establish the tone and affirmation of the goals as to why you are meeting today. Prepare these statements ahead of time, so they are not loose in their interpretation nor vague in what you are trying to communicate. You want to be clear in YOUR mind to the purpose of this gathering so you can communicate it clearly to THEIR minds.

Once you have established the main priorities, you can move ahead with the issues to be discussed and agreements to the next activities. To keep a balance, integrating action and assessment, follow the simple pattern:

Prepare - Act - Review - Prepare . . .

In this way, you will never have paralysis by analysis. The worst aspect of delaying any action is not missing an opportunity. Delaying action hurts the quality of the work, because there is no chance to learn how to improve it before the job is done. Prepare, then act, then review, then prepare again.

Fourth: Create Peer Pressure. Peer pressure is something
we were all taught to avoid in junior high school. "Don't let your friends influence you to do what you shouldn't," would be the battle cry of our teachers and parents during these impressionable years. Peer pressure was the subversive game plan of those who wanted us

to try smoking, drinking or other activities youngsters shouldn't be
doing.

In the adult world, peer pressure is something we can, and should,
create in order to formulate a new norm to advance your revolution.
Peer pressure is effective with bosses who are ignoring your ideas,
as well as with co-workers who are more reluctant to join in. Peer
pressure is much more effective than bullying, intimidating or the
option many of us immediately jump to when our ideas are not being
acted on as quickly as we think, which is to leap-frog over our
immediate supervisor and go over his head. Doing this will most
likely damage your relationship in the process, making future
requests almost impossible. Rather than going to your boss's boss,
first give extra effort to apply peer pressure through the following
techniques:

   1) **You must be the first to follow-up.** Many of us make a
request, but then never follow-up to see if it is being acted upon.
When we don't return to ask about the status of our idea or what
action steps have been implemented, we are sending the message
that it really wasn't that important. Apparently, our idea doesn't have
much merit if we don't feel it is worth asking about again. Follow-
up. Let a few days pass, then ask what is happening concerning your
previous conversation.

Which leads us to the reason many of our requests are ignored or go
unheeded--because we approach our supervisor or co-worker
looking to have a *confrontation* rather than a *conversation*. A
conversation will reap great rewards in getting your ideas
implemented. A confrontation only places the other party in a
position to defend himself and his own ideas, rather than include
yours.

When you approach someone, continually think **Conversation** not
Confrontation. The difference is:

Conversation	Confrontation
Begin with a positive attitude	Begin with an irritated attitude
Use a friendly tone of voice	Use an aggressive tone of voice
Stick to the facts	Use their personality traits to attack
Offer solutions	Submit problems
Have an idea	Have an excuse
Say, "let me help"	"Not my job"
See an answer for every problem	See a problem with every answer
"It may be difficult, yet possible."	"It may be possible, but its too difficult."
The goal is to achieve results and have future conversations	The goal is winning at all costs

2) **Be specific.** When you talk in generalities, it allows loop holes as to why something isn't being done. Be specific with time (what day, week or month), with action steps (what are the explicit activities planned), with people (who precisely is doing what), with accountability measurements (how will we definitively know progress is being made). Expanded material on the need for specificity is presented in Step 5: Increase Commitment, where information is outlined on how to get anyone to do anything. Being specific with your conversations will avoid misinterpretations, wrong assumptions, and foggy expectations of each party.

3) **Take three or four of your co-workers to witness the conversation.** Going alone to your supervisor presents an automatic power imbalance against you. If you are alone, then it's his word against yours. Peer pressure means that more than two people are

witnesses to agreements and action steps. When you have multiple bodies in the room, it creates an unstated obligation to appease more than just a single individual. Bring along three or four others who will be affected by the implementation of your idea. Let your cohorts contribute their voice of support and willingness to participate in the solution. The goal is NOT to gang up on your boss. This will only generate resentment towards you and hamper future efforts at peer pressure.

The goal is to create a friendly, cooperative atmosphere wherein everyone feels comfortable expressing their thoughts and feelings about an issue or topic. Converse not confront.

4) **Take your idea to a peer or management team.** If the first three steps result in no action, then take your idea to a team meeting. The team, whether within a department or managerial staff meeting, will also act as group peer pressure with unstated accountability attached. Your supervisor is now aware that not only you will be asking about your idea, but so will your peers at the next staff meeting. You now have pressure from multiple sides, all of it amicable and, still, all of it moving your idea through to completion.

With each of these steps, review and apply the principles of *persistence* versus being a *pest,* as again presented in the next chapter on Increase Commitment. You will need to be persistent if you feel your idea has merit and can contribute to a positive environment. But, as soon as you are perceived as being a pest, the road to your revolution becomes much bumpier.

Mantra vs. Mission Statements

 Every company I have ever consulted with, worked for or walked in to has had a mission statement. They are usually printed on bright white or cream colored paper, professionally and beautifully framed, hanging in the front entryway or lobby for all to see. They contain universal truth words such as "quality," "integrity," and "nurturing environment." These mission statements also contain the words, "customer," employees," and "endeavor."

Still, I have yet to find one single person, including any CEO, manager, or supervisor, let alone anyone who actually performs the front line work, able to repeat the mission statement without reading it--if they can find it. When asked, "Do you have a mission statement?", they will universally say, yes. "Tell it to me" is always met with embarrassed silence or falteringly, worn-out statements such as "quality people, quality products, doing our utmost for the customer," etc., etc., ad nauseam.

NO one, and I'll repeat, No ONE has ever been able to tell me the mission statement of their company. Why is that? I've attended shop meetings where everyone reads it together out loud. I've stood in the office of CEOs where their walls are lined, not only with their ornately framed mission statement (I've noticed their frames are more expensive and elaborate than the one in the lobby), but also inspiring odes to health, wealth and the pursuit of corporeal fulfillment. But can they repeat any of these back to me? NO.

Mission statements are created by a group of well-intentioned, upper management sorts who went to a nice resort for a weekend in order to establish purpose and direction for their company. Thrown into the mix are words of exemplar individual and corporate behavior, along with utopia-like working conditions where we are all brothers and sisters, standing side-by-side in the quest for optimal personal and collective performance on behalf of an entity known affectionately as--the customer. Mission statements are long, unintelligible and fail to accomplish their intended purpose: to rally the minds of all working to a single thought that will help them perform their jobs better.

How can it help when no one can remember it! Here is a prime,
real-life example.

> **"We are an independent financial resource dedicated to
> honoring our core values as we build successful long-
> term relationships with employees, individuals, families
> and enterprises in the markets we serve and with the
> shareholders who have provided the capital for us to
> thrive."**

Wow! That's a mouthful. It sounds impressive. Tell me, of what
value is that statement if a customer is asking me for a little extra
help after I have punched out for the day? How can it help if: A) I
can't remember it, and B) I don't understand it?

I know I sound like someone who thinks we shouldn't have mission
statements along with corresponding principles and values. Not true.
I do think they have the potential purpose of setting a course and
direction that can guide a company as a whole to what they wish to
achieve. Generally.

The main failure of a mission statement is we have substituted it as
the holy grail, and we point to it as the only means of guidance.
During the course of every working day, individuals must make
decisions on how they will act or respond to a given set of
circumstances. What will guide their thought process in order to
make the correct decision? How can we use the mission statement
when THEY CAN'T EVEN REMEMBER IT? How can it guide our
decision-making process while I'm standing in front of a customer
who is yelling at me about some broken part when I don't know
where to find it in order to re-read it? How can it direct my thoughts
and actions when co-workers are battling over who will work this
Saturday if I can only muster memories of "quality" and "integrity,"
but nothing that has ANY meaning to right here -- right now?

Mission statements have become an institutionalized part of our corporate culture. "Institutionalized" means no one has to think about it. An institutionalized criminal will not walk into the next room, but instead pause at the threshold of a door until given permission to enter. They no longer think about their choices; they just do what they have been conditioned to do.

For a revolution to take root, take hold, anchor deep, we must uninstitutionalize our thought process and that of others. We must find a way to guide the actions and thoughts of others toward a single, unifying goal while at the same time, setting them free to think and be creative with their individual choices to achieve that commonly held goal. The answer is found in your MANTRA.

A mantra accomplishes these purposes:
❑   A mantra can be remembered.
❑   A mantra is used to help guide a person to make a proper decision based on a proper thought.
❑   A mantra is truly unifying because every person is capable of achieving its ideal, making it the perfect answer to any question.

Your company should have one over-riding mantra that sets the tone and direction for what you want to achieve. After that, each department might have its own mantra that dovetails with the specific tasks they perform each day, guiding them to achieve the company mantra.

You might have a mantra to guide thoughts and actions to achieve a specific behavioral goal within the organization. For example, a foundry with over 100 employees felt the need for greater cooperation between its workforce and departments. There seemed to be continuous contention and friction that wasn't healthy or productive. One long-time worker went so far as to say that hate for your fellow employee was the norm. They created a mantra to guide their thoughts and actions to attain greater cooperation and, as a result, conversations became more productive. More work was actually completed rather than fighting about who did what.

A mantra can serve many purposes for the express reason that it works in ALL situations when rallying a group of people to a common thought. Here are the rules for an effective mantra:

◈ *A mantra must be ten words or less.* Why? Then people can remember it!

The company who wished to generate greater cooperation between its employees created a mantra that started a revolution. They created:

**I demonstrate positive actions and attitudes
with all my co-workers.**

Fantastic! Just imagine the possibilities for everyone within a company having this one common thought to help guide them and make correct decisions on what to do. The next day, the union shop steward posted this mantra on his toolbox as a reminder to himself and for all others to see -- this was the new standard (also excellent Modeling Behavior from step 1!). Outstanding! It doesn't matter your position or role, personal or professional, within a company or a family or church or any organization. A mantra you can remember has the opportunity to guide your actions and attitudes.

A hotel in Jacksonville, Florida has this mantra posted next to the check-in counter:

Every Customer leaves Satisfied!

There you have it. Simple. Direct. Anyone can make any decision, no matter what their position, based on that mantra. Here is an even greater challenge. See if you can whittle it down, like this hotel, to six words or less. Not only will it be even more memorable, it will also bring a sharper focus to what you stand for and what you are trying to accomplish. The more you can narrow the thought pattern, shaving and peeling the extraneous away to where only the most concise and precise language is used, the easier you will find people applying it to their everyday, every hour situations.

✧ *A mantra must be doable by anyone.*
Often, mission statements include directives that are out of the control of many of the employees. Only top management can make a difference in these particular areas of command. So how is this a motivator for the other 99% of employees? The mantra is something EVERYONE can do at anytime and can act as a guide to ANY daily decision that arises. The words must have meaning to each individual. It must become personal and practical, or it won't have any affect at all.

A study was done at Yale University where a professor wanted to see if he could persuade a group of college seniors to get tetanus shots. He divided them into two groups and gave each group a seven-page booklet explaining the dangers of tetanus, the importance of inoculation, and the fact that the University was offering free tetanus shots at the campus health center to all interested students.

When the students were later given a questionnaire, all the students appeared to be well-educated about the dangers of tetanus. However, one month later, almost NONE of the subjects - a mere 3% - had actually gone to the health center to get inoculated. The lessons learned by the students had been forgotten and did not translate into action.

One small change was made in a subsequent experiment. Along with the "fear" booklet on the dangers of tetanus, there was included a map of the campus with the university health building circled with times that the shots were available clearly listed. The vaccination rate - the response rate - jumped to 28%! The students needed to know how to fit the tetanus information into their everyday lives; the addition of the map and times when the shots were available shifted the booklet from an abstract lesson in medical risk - no different from countless other academic lessons they received over their college experience - to a practical and personal piece of medical advice.

Once the advice became personal and practical, it became memorable and doable by everyone.

✧ *A mantra must move through time.*
It doesn't change with the rolling trends of economy, boom or bust. It isn't dependent on a certain type of employee or even a particular kind of manager. That's because a mantra is focused on behavior and our interaction and response to a swirling set of ever-changing circumstances, not on our internal bias or reflexive auto-pilot rebuttal. A universal mantra is not bound by policy and procedure manuals. A mantra demands that a person think and act upon the mantra, not a management dictum.

The mantra of the Edmonton, Alberta, police department is:

Committed to Community Needs

Notice it doesn't state what specific need -- just the need, whatever it is, in their particular community at that particular moment in time. The law enforcement officer who shared that mantra with me said, "We had to make a decision. Were we going to be keepers of the law or keepers of the peace? The answer will affect the decisions you make in your everyday work life."

He went on to illustrate how an officer pulled an erratic driver off to the side of the road for veering from side-to-side. The driver could be drunk or under the influence of drugs or any number of illegal reasons to produce this unstable, meandering driving. But when the officer walked up alongside the door, he noticed the man was crying. The driver explained that he just found out his wife had cancer and would, in all probability, die very shortly. His mind and thoughts were obviously in a different place than in this car. The officer talked to him briefly and let the man go home.

What, in this case, is the purpose of the police officer: to keep the law or keep the peace? When you are committed to community needs, the answer becomes exceedingly clear.

Make your mantra a cornerstone of your revolution. All actions and decisions are tested against the mantra: consistent or contradictory? Without it, you and your people will be adrift to whims, emotions and temporal circumstances that may change at a moment's notice.

How to Create Your Mantra

When I first took ownership of WGEZ, an AM radio station in southern Wisconsin, it had three employees and was losing $10,000 cash every month. Not accounting losses--real cash money losses. We met in my sparse apartment on Bluff Street, sitting on the floor with only a pillow and a bean bag chair to share. I stood before them and simply asked, "So what do you want to do?"

They looked at me with blank stares. "What do you mean? You're the new owner. You tell us what you want done."

"No, you don't understand. This is OUR company. I may be the owner, but this is OUR company. This is a once-in-a-lifetime opportunity to build something we can be proud of. What would you like to do?"

And we began to throw out phrases and words that described how we wanted to build a company and interact with each and our customers. Phrases like "people being most important," "doing the right thing," "having fun," "showing respect," "helping our customers succeed, "etc. From this emerged our mantra -- our guiding force for making all decisions:

> *People over product*
> *Always take the high road*
> *Have Fun while doing it.*

It was memorable (less than ten words when you take out the subjunctive words to make it logical). It was doable, and it was timeless. This mantra defined who we wanted to be, how we wished to act, and the environment we wanted to live and work in. It gave us a personality outside ourselves that complimented our individual values and principles. This is the essence of what a mantra can do for a company and its people.

Here is how to create your mantra. Have poster board or an easel pad and markers so you can work out your mantra in full view.

FIRST: *Write 2-3 sentences describing their ideal.* You may wish to have it broad-based, such as your ideal company. Or you may be more specific and describe how you wish to treat your customer or treat each other. Have each person write it out. Take your time. This is important. Speed is not the objective. It's everyone's opportunity to create his or her own working and living environment. Two, three or four sentences are all that's needed.

SECOND: *Each person circle the theme word or words from each sentence.* Reading through the phrases describing their ideal, words will begin to pop out -- theme words that embrace the concept of the whole sentence. Have them circle these words on their paper. With this technique, you are helping them to distill their thoughts smaller and smaller until you get down to the essence of their ideal -- their core.

THIRD: *Each person reads his sentences out loud.* As each sentence is read slowly, one sentence at a time, occasionally two or three times over, have the group give their opinions as to what the key word or words are, and write them on the easel pad. The person reading his sentence can add his key words if he choses something different, but usually, the key words selected will be very similar.

FOURTH: *Link the words that have common meaning.* These are the key themes that everyone is commonly thinking. They're conceiving the same thought, but using different words to describe it. Circle these words on the pad and transfer them over to a clean sheet in order to form a logical phrase or word grouping. It's important, as a leader, that you guide them to these key thoughts without telling them what they should say. The object isn't to put words in their mouth, but to show them the commonality of their ideal.

FIFTH: *Keep reducing the word group.* Continue to hone the number of words into a sharply focused action phrase of 10 words or less. Mix the words around. Take out any word that is not needed to help explain the whole. Sharper and sharper. Make it personal. Test your word grouping with a real-life situation by asking yourself, "Does this phrase help guide someone to make the correct decision?"

Is it specific enough? Get to the heart, the very core of your idea. Make it succinct and so crystal clear that no one could misinterpret it, even if they tried. Once you have tested your word grouping with several scenarios and circumstances and everyone can say, "Yes, this group of words will guide me to make a proper decision," then you have your mantra.

Congratulations! You have taken a monumental step towards launching your revolution. Your group of people, no matter how large or small, can now rally around a single thought, and it will lead them to effective thought patterns and activities. But, you're not quite done.

SIXTH: *Communicate your mantra.* Plan how you will distribute and execute your mantra among every person in every department. DO NOT COMMUNICATE YOUR MANTRA WITHOUT FIRST EXPLAINING THE REASON AND PURPOSE BEHIND IT! If you do, you will be <u>telling</u> them without <u>asking</u> for their buy-in to the ideal purpose. You must first show them how the end purpose has personal benefit before they will commit to the ideal.

Only after your presentation and explanation of how the ideal purpose has meaning to their individual lives, THEN you may distribute the mantra as a guide to fulfilling that purpose. You can do this in a number of ways:

- ▶▶ A company-wide meeting for one gigantic roll-out.

- ▶▶ Small team meetings within each department with a manager who was involved in the creation process acting as facilitator.

- ▶▶ One-on-one teaching and coaching of how the mantra works in their specific situations.

- ▶▶ Fliers, posters, buttons and banners as visual symbols of the mantra.

▶ T-shirts, hats and armbands that proclaim the mantra.

▶ Print the mantra on all company or departmental paperwork.

▶ Verbal affirmation of the mantra at subsequent meetings -- shout it out!

▶ Public press release to the media and celebration kick-off.

▶ A marketing piece sent to every customer explaining the purpose and benefit of the mantra in their relationship to your company.

One company even re-landscaped the front entryway to include their mantra spelled out in colored stones for everyone to see. What a proclamation of their values and purpose -- reaffirmed on a daily basis with all employees and customers.

Use your imagination to create unique and impactful ways to communicate the mantra to all corners of your operation.

Then don't lose sight of it.

When decisions are made, test them to the mantra -- consistent or contradictory?

When conversations become heated, test the process to the mantra -- consistent or contradictory?

When opportunities arise to make a change, test the idea to the mantra -- consistent or contradictory?

Kelly was a new assistant, recently hired to help our front office manager. Kelly was a bright, young lady, but had never worked in an environment where the policy and procedure manual wasn't the

Bible for her thought process. In fact, in past jobs, she rarely had to make a decision. She just consulted the policy or, not finding it in time, didn't do anything.

We taught her our mantra:

> People over Product
> Always take the High Road
> Have Fun while doing it

She was taught to apply this mantra to any given situation, whether her supervisor or I was present or not. She had the power to make decisions based on our mantra.

I had returned from an extended road trip and was sitting in my office when I heard a soft knock on the door. Kelly shuffled in, stood in front of my desk and, with her head bowed down quietly, said, "Remember how you told us you'd support us no matter what decision we made?"

This is not a good way to start a conversation!

"Yes, Kelly, tell me the story. What happened?"

"Well, this customer came in while you were gone and he was SOOOOO mad. He was shouting and swearing. He had purchased a satellite dish on the Shopping Show program and it didn't work. And he wanted 100% of his money back. So . . . (thinking 'People over Product') I refunded 100% of his money. Was that okay?"

"I don't' know, Kelly. I wasn't here. Was the customer happy?"

"Well, I wanted our customer to be happy with us so . . . (thinking 'always take the high road') I refunded 100% of his money, AND I gave him a coupon for 20% off his next Shopping Show purchase.

Was that okay?"

Again, I said, "I don't know, Kelly. Was the customer happy?"

"Well . . ." -- her hesitancy quickly forming an ulcer in my stomach. Oh my . . . what did she do! Loan out my house for a weekend junket for this guy?

"I wanted our customer to be really, really happy with us so . . . (thinking "have fun while doing it") I refunded 100% of his money, gave him a 20% off coupon and . . . I wrote a check for $50 for him to take his wife out to dinner for the inconvenience. Was that okay?"

Believe me, I didn't want to ask again, but I had no choice!

"I don't know, Kelly. Was the customer happy?"

Her face lit up, her eyes sparkled as she squealed, "He was SOOOOO happy, he was laughing and smiling and he said 'you guys can screw up anytime you want!" And he became a customer for life and has since spent tens of thousands of dollars on the Shopping Show. And what do you think this guy was talking about to his wife as they enjoyed a dinner on us?

"Kelly. You did perfect. Good job." And she twirled on her toes, bounced out of my office, and went back to her desk with full acknowledgment that she had done the right thing. She was capable and empowered, because the mantra had guided her thoughts to make the correct decision. Without the mantra, she would be debating conflicting thoughts like, "Will Steve approve? Am I allowed to do this? What if the customer stays mad at me?"

Instead, the mantra was her road map. The mantra pointed her down the correct path.

The mantra expanded our revolution.

As it can yours.

Revolutionary Tactics to Build A Coalition

➡ Choose one other person and share your vision. Then each of you choose two others to join your revolutionary goal.

➡ Elicit input from every person on your team.

➡ Consult before deciding. Ask questions rather than telling. Incorporate the ideas of others and require participation from all.

➡ Consistently schedule times to exchange information. Be sure each meeting has:
>   A purpose
>   Proper thinking
>   Learning
>   Engagement
>   The opportunity for feedback for continuous improvement.

➡ Create peer pressure by:
>   Following up yourself first
>   Being specific with your request
>   Bring others as witnesses
>   Present your idea to a team or staff meeting

➡ Create a mantra to guide daily decisions and thought patterns. Make it:
>   Ten words or less
>   Doable by everyone
>   Movable through time
>   Understandable by linking key theme words
>   Heard by everyone throughout the organization

➡ Test all decisions, policies and objectives to the mantra. Is it consistent or contradictory?

STEP 4 Manage The Change
STEP 3 Build A Coalition
STEP 2 Establish Your Goal
STEP 1 Set Your Foundation

Step 4: Manage the Change

"Difficulty is the excuse history never accepts."

A company, feeling it is time for a shakeup, hires a new CEO. The new boss is determined to rid the company of all slackers. On a tour of the facilities, the CEO notices a guy leaning against a wall. The room is full of workers, and he wants them to know he means business! The CEO walks up to the guy and asks, "And how much money do you make a week?"

Undaunted, the young fellow looks at him and replies, "I make $200 a week. Why?"

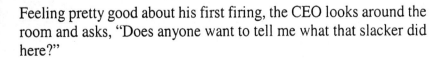

The CEO hands him $200 in cash and screams, "Here's a weeks pay! Now GET OUT and don't come back!" Surprisingly, the guy takes the cash with a smile saying, "Yes, sir! Thank you, sir!" and leaves.

Feeling pretty good about his first firing, the CEO looks around the room and asks, "Does anyone want to tell me what that slacker did here?"

With a sheepish grin, one of the workers mutters, "Pizza delivery guy from Dominos."

Hopefully your revolution won't begin like this clueless CEO's! Once you have created the foundation of your revolution setting your foundation, establishing your goal and beginning to build your coalition of like-minded people who, together, create a mantra to guide your decision making process, there comes a time when someone will challenge your attempt to make positive changes.

Some changes you will plan for, others will happen on their own. Some changes will be good, such as an upswing in attitude and the level of contribution from others. Other changes may be less desirable, such as extreme counter-actions with outright defiance or bulldozing ideas and activities that aren't compatible with your primary goal. There will be those who don't get what your revolution is all about and deride you by saying, "Nothing will ever change around here. Why are you knocking yourself out? For what? You're crazy."

In every field of human endeavor, he that is first must perpetually live in the white light of publicity. When a man's work becomes a standard for the whole world, it also becomes a target for the shafts of the envious few. If his work is merely mediocre, he will be left severely alone. If he achieves a masterpiece, he will set a million tongues awagging. Long, long after a great work has been done, those who are disappointed or envious continue to cry out that it cannot be done. Failing to equal or excel, the follower seeks to depreciate and to destroy, but only confirms once more the superiority of that which he strives to supplant.

There is nothing new in this. It is as old as the world and as old as the human passions of envy, fear, greed, ambition and desire to surpass. If the leader truly leads, he remains the leader. That which deserves to live - lives.

Change is going to come, one way or the other. Take heart and understand the origins of frustration which could derail you from your intended goal. The three sources of frustration include:

> Expectations that are not fulfilled
> An intention is blocked
> Feelings about a situation are not communicated

Expectations that are not fulfilled. If you make an appointment with Bob and you expect him to be on time and he fails to show up or give any advance notice of his delay, you will feel a degree of frustration, negative emotion. When you expect someone to complete his task in an acceptable manner, or simply do what he agreed to do, it doesn't take long for you to become exasperated.

An intention is blocked. John decides to reward his highly productive team members with a bonus. He will feel thwarted if someone in Human Resources states that this is not company policy, yet, fails to suggest an alternative. Even though John understands that the HR person is just citing policy, he is still likely to see HR as a barrier to what he believes is a valid tribute.

Feelings about a situation are not communicated. If your boss does not review the status of your project as promised and fails to authorize the initiation of the next phase, the resulting confusion and delays will likely cause an emotional reaction on your part. Yet, even though people get upset in situations like these, they often avoid telling their boss how they feel. Instead, they withhold their feelings and choose not to communicate what has happened. Holding back often fuels feelings of anger or resentment, and these emotions can damage the relationship if left unchecked and unspoken.

When you recognize frustration building, ask yourself if it was triggered by (1) unmet expectations, (2) blocked intentions, or (3) your own undelivered communication about the situation. Leaders who have learned how to resolve their own conflicts and manage the elements of frustration are more likely to be able to coach others on how to effectively deal with similar feelings and situations. Teaching people how to diminish or eliminate their sources of frustration, combined with the skills of conflict resolution, can improve productivity, collaboration and morale.

> One of the true tests of leadership is the ability to recognize a problem before it becomes one.

Here, then, is your choice: accept the fact that hiccups will inevitably occur, someone will get his nose out of joint because he wasn't invited to the revolution first, while others will just ignore you altogether. Or fight these battles at every turn. If you choose to fight -- you will burn out. If you choose to accept, then you can prepare and present a more effective response. The Art of War teaches us that if we fight in anger, we will fight bravely and lose quickly. Don't lose your cool; instead, take a new view of these periods of change.

The Chinese character for "crisis" is, incidentally, one which means "dangerous opportunity." The danger is in not recognizing the opportunity within change and then failing to respond with appropriate teaching. The danger is attempting to persist with the old "Command and Control" style of leadership.

Command and Control includes:

Assume shared meanings of words, goals and objectives.
The aim is to control uncertainty.
Attain the ability to predict.
Interpret events in order to stabilize the environment.

Managers today are under the illusion that they know, more or less, what's going to happen next or how people will react. That's both arrogant and dangerous. Not only do those managers ignore the possibility that something unexpected will happen, they also forget that the decisions they do make can have unintended consequences.

Consider the launch of New Coke in 1985. Immediately after the product was introduced, the company got as many as 8,000 letters a day from angry customers. Clearly, Coca-Cola had failed to accurately predict people's behavior. The story shows, you have to take action at the earliest sign of danger or you may get killed. Everyday problems escalate to disaster status very quickly when people don't respond appropriately to signs of trouble.

The more effective style of response to change is called the "River Method." Just as a river bends and turns with the shores and banks it encounters, so, too, the "River Method" continuously bends and adapts to each circumstance. The river does not attempt to control its environment but, rather, seeks to blend and integrate itself to the advantage of both.

The River Method includes:

*Recognizing emerging behavior and act with
    a timely response.
Communicate guidelines while searching for
    non-obvious or indirect solutions.
Attain the ability to be flexible, adaptable and creative.
Interpret events to blend with the environment we choose.*

Do you see the importance of anticipating reaction to change . . .
good and not so good? You can annul a number of the pessimistic
responses with effective and continuous "SCANing." *Effective*
means "with proper technique resulting in a favorable outcome," and
continuous means "don't stop!" If you effectively and continuously
"SCAN" your employees and co-workers, you can avoid what is
called a cosmology episode.

A cosmology episode is the opposite of a deja vu experience. In
moments of deja vu, everything suddenly feels familiar,
recognizable. By contrast, in a cosmology episode, everything seems
strange. A person feels like he has never been here before, has no
idea of where he is ,and has no idea who can help him. An inevitable
state of panic ensues, and the individual becomes more and more
anxious until he finds it impossible to make sense of what is
happening.

The continual merging and divesting and recombining and changing
of responsibilities and bosses over the years has created intense
cosmological episodes for many businesses. Compound these
conditions with globalization and high-velocity change and nobody
seems to have a firm sense of who they really are and where they fit
in. Many people even have trouble locating themselves on an
organizational chart!

The resulting emotions include fear, paranoia, depression, rage,
apathy, isolation, indifference, and resignation. What we need to do
is alter the following equation:

Anxiety + Fear = Anguish
(resulting in dread, reluctance
  and exhaustion)

And change it to:

Anxiety + Hope = Anticipation
(resulting in commitment, excitement
  and exhilaration)

The answer to this dilemma is to effectively and continuously SCAN.

SCAN

Specifics. Specifically describe what is changing and why. Broad generalities that can be loosely interpreted will cause frustration, agitation and anger. The rumor mill will never be obliterated, but its affects can be negated when you share facts to mix with the talk. Be specific.

Concerns. Address the concerns of each individual whether, in your view, valid or invalid. These concerns will be on their minds and talked about so, again, the best course of action is to discuss them outright. Just as you can't clean garbage out of a pond unless you first bring it to the surface, so, too, you must bring these concerns to the surface and handle them with dialog that is direct, honest and frank.

Attitudes. Anticipate the attitudes that will be directed toward the change. These need to be met with the same candor as their concerns. Problematic attitudes can be positive or negative. A positive attitude may be someone who is overzealous and tend to jump ahead of the curve, changing this or that prior to your time table. A negative attitude is obviously difficult because, unchecked, it can unhinge all your efforts, sometimes without you even knowing it. Deal with each attitude privately, one-on-one. This will allow you to be more direct and honest than in a group setting.

Needs. What needs are required to successfully complete your change? Needs will fall into each of the following four areas: physical, social, rewards and information. Physical needs could assess the use of space and equipment. Social needs might deal with the level personality cohesiveness and managerial input. Rewards are knowing what moves individuals to act such as compensation, time off and self-esteem. Information needs include time lines, budgets and the projected goals.

Continuously be SCANing your team, and you will foresee any hindrances to be avoided or constructive territories to spend time improving. While SCANing is an effective evaluative tool, and you may think you're on track with the mind set of each team member, you will never have all your bases covered unless you consider a small, seemingly insignificant radio station that could override all your best intended efforts. That radio station is:

WIIFM

A large portion of the change process has to do with a radio station WII-FM. As you are instructing about the elements of the upcoming change, there will be times when your students are not listening. They have inadvertently (or maybe on purpose) tuned you out. Your voice begins to sound like the speaker box in a Charlie Brown cartoon; wha wha, wha, wha. The squawking is an irritant to their ears, and they are no longer learning.

That's because that little radio station in the back of all our minds has kicked in, and we must address our attention to that new, little voice. We each have it, and we each listen to it on a regular basis. WII-FM

What's In It For Me

A revolution, personal or involving others, must always address -- what's in it for me. In other words, addressing the personal application and benefit for a particular action or responsibility. Why should they do what you are requesting? Why should anyone do anything? You will build confidence and motivation when you continually point out the individual and group benefits for doing what we are doing, learning what we are learning. Everyone is thinking it. You might as well address it so it doesn't become a hindrance to further instruction.

Most people will respond to change when it addresses their individual, personal needs. Those needs may be real or perceived, but they are believed to be true within that individual. Cults are formed because of real or perceived needs that are being met by a charismatic leader, needs for family, belonging, purpose. These are real needs, whether they are met with legitimacy and positive results or false claims and destructive consequences.

Always address the needs of others first. This will lend credibility to your revolution. If its about **you** first, there will be doubt as to your own motives and actions. Talk about what THEY would like accomplish within this setting, and the WIIFM will be tuned into the group and its ultimate purpose.

Once you have addressed the needs of others first, do remember to take care of yourself as well. Apply the following tips, and you'll find yourself in better shape for handling the uncertainties of change:

Don't make today's circumstances tomorrow's sacred cows. What happens today is today. Tomorrow is a new game and new opportunity to make a difference.

Keep listening and communicating. It's too easy in times of extreme change to withdraw and avoid. It's sometimes easier than facing reality. Make every attempt to stay in tune -- stay in touch and keep talking.

Get a new perspective. At times, all we need is a different point of view. Take a walk, talk to a friend, read a novel. Just get your mind into a dissimilar state than you're presently dealing with. New doors of thought and alternatives will open.

Surround yourself with and utilize champions. Others have traveled this path. Talk to them. Get their advice and counsel. Tap into their expertise and experience. It'll help just knowing you're not alone and, more than likely, you'll find an answer faster than by yourself.

Build skills of self-observation and correction. Your greatest asset is yourself. our greatest enemy is . . . yourself. Be aware of what is happening within and without (review the signs of frustration). What are you feeling? What is happening? What do you desire to happen? What steps need to be taken to steer you to that desired outcome? Take those steps.

Upon hearing about fields of diamonds in a foreign land, an old farmer sold all his possessions to search for his riches. After years of searching his land over and over again, the farmer died broken and bankrupt. Soon after, a neighbor passing by, saw a glint shining off a rock. With a bit of digging, the neighbor had discovered, that just below the surface were, to what the farmer looked like, ordinary rocks. But with the proper cutting, chipping and polishing, these ordinary rocks were actually some of the world's most priceless gems.

The farmer owned his field of diamonds all along. If he had only looked just below the surface to see the jewels he already had in his possession.

Use this "dangerous opportunity" of change to mine a few diamonds of your own to put in your back pocket.

Revolutionary Tactics to Manage the Change

➡ Recognize the 3 sources of frustration and address them when managing change:
   Expectations are not fulfilled
   An intention is blocked
   Feelings are nt communicated

➡ Use the "River Method" when facing change:
   Bend, adapt, flex and create new options
   Search for non-obvious and indirect solutions
   Interpret events to blend with the environment we *choose*.

➡ Continuously SCAN:
   Specific information is communicated
   Concerns, real or perceived, are addressed
   Attitudes are anticipated
   Needs are met for success

➡ Address the issue of WIIFM up front: What's In It For ME?
   Attend to the needs of others first
   Keep listening and communicating
   Get a fresh perspective
   Surround yourself and utilize champions
   Build skills of self-obsession and correction

STEP 5 Increase Commitment
STEP 4 Manage The Change
STEP 3 Build A Coalition
STEP 2 Establish Your Goal
STEP 1 Set Your Foundation

Step 5: Increase Commitment

My beloved Green Bay Packers have begun another football season. Sunday gatherings will now be timed and executed with precision to work around the kick-off and its subsequent yelling, bemoaning, referee-bashing, exhilaration and sometimes disappointment. I have noticed, however, when watching both teams sprint out onto the field, they all act exactly the same. They chant and cheer and raise their arms in a circle. They crash helmets, pound pads, grunting and growling with the fierceness of war-hungry combatants. Putting on their "game face."

If you substituted their individually brightly colored uniforms with a generic, earth-tone dye, you wouldn't be able to tell the teams apart. Both have equal motivation for winning, both have intensity and a sincere belief they are going to emerge from the battle victorious. They run around the sidelines alike, kick the ball with matching accuracy, and swap tales of glorious past games.

The clock ticks down, zeros blink across the scoreboard, the whistle sounds and the teams sprint back into the tunnel, down into their locker room for the celebration and jubilation of a day well-spent.

No?

What's wrong with this picture? You mean the teams don't just rush back into the locker room? Why not? What's missing?

The game!

Oh, the game is missing. The game must be played. It's not enough for the teams to get all dressed up, act like they're having fun, dance around a bit and then call it a day. If they were paid to do just that -- none of this broken bones, smashing teeth stuff -- I would be the first in line to don the uniform. For less money than they make now, to boot!

The game must always be played for the preparation, the training and the goal setting to have any meaning or validity. Otherwise, it was an exercise in futility that may have made us feel good about ourselves, but without any lasting value or contribution to the greater good. To play the game is the culmination of everything that preceded it -- it's the true face of commitment. It's what we do, what we successfully execute that matters, and will ultimately be the historical judge of who "wins."

Gaining commitment to any new idea is one of the more challenging aspects of starting a revolution. After all, this is a revolution, something others may have imagined, but you are the first to actually do something about it. The idea of a revolution may not be new, but now that it could be a reality, it can scare some people off. Creating commitment is a skill that is a necessary part of any group dynamic if a change is to last longer than just through the initial emotional surge. People love change, when it doesn't affect them!

Commitment is created through the backdoor. Commitment is something that takes time. Deep commitment comes from the heart and soul of a person, not through the public rally cry of "let's do something." Commitment is personal. It takes tactful skill to create any level of commitment in each individual. Commitment may be voiced within the environment of a group, but it takes root in the one-on-one interaction you have with the people who you want as a part of your reformation.

Commitment is accomplished through a process, not unlike the sales process. You are, after all, selling an idea. You are taking a suspicious prospect and turning him into your committed customer. Commitment starts slowly and progresses step by step through five stages.

5 Stages of Commitment Cycle

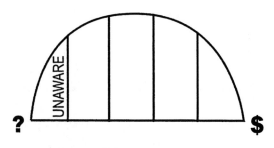

Stage #1: Unaware

Unawareness simply means a person is uninformed to what it is you are trying to accomplish. He may know *you* on some level, but he is unaware of your goals or intention. He is not for or against you, he is just unaware.

You would rather begin from this stage than to battle negative misperceptions from past mistakes or ill-informed and misguided managers who left a legacy of suspicion, or possibly contempt. Multi-generationally owned companies many times have to fight the past ghosts before they can move forward. One such owner was a third generation son who, in front of his workers, apologized for his forefathers and those who had created an atmosphere of hatred within the company. His workers applauded his comments, and now they prepared to move ahead.

Unaware is the first stage of the commitment process. You will now move your prospects to the second stage.

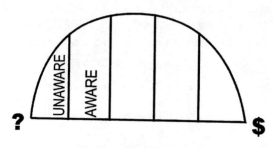

Stage #2: Aware

At the second stage, your co-worker or teammates have been made aware that you are starting something exciting. They are still not for or against the idea, they are just now aware of who you are and a surface level familiarity that you are up to something. Maybe they were talking with a mutual acquaintance at the water cooler or in the cafeteria, or the rumor mill is simply starting to crank up. They mentioned your name and that you were having a meeting about making some important changes. They may be intrigued enough to seek you out and ask you some questions; they may not. But at least they are aware that something is afoot.

The third stage of commitment is where it begins to get interesting.

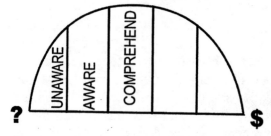

Stage #3: Comprehend

Comprehension is defined as:

"I understand what a product, service or idea can do."

This is the rational stage of commitment. Someone who is interested will begin to ask questions, do some research, try to find out what's going on. Or you may be talking with someone, telling them about your idea. Their eyes light up, indicating, "tell me more." This is the "facts and figures" part of the revolution. What exactly is your goal? Who exactly is going to be involved? When are you going to begin? Where will the meeting be held? These questions must be answered if anyone is going to join your efforts to make a change and make a difference. They are not emotionally involved, just logically curious, looking for some answers to basic inquiries.

They still haven't bought your idea. They are not yet committed. They are on the outside looking in. Yet, this is the most critical moment. This is when most revolutions drop into oblivion. This is when change is stopped, momentum is halted, all because we misunderstand this stage of the commitment process.

We tend to think that if people KNOW what we are doing and they UNDERSTAND the facts of what we are trying to accomplish, they should just naturally want to jump on the bandwagon. They should WANT to be involved. Why aren't they joining our little band of rebels by the droves? Why are they holding back? I've told them what we're doing! Can't they see how great this is going to be?

No, they can't – for the simple reason we have not moved them to the fourth stage of commitment. There is no commitment, no buy-in, no matter how hard we try to explain ourselves or how logically beneficial this all may seems to us. Nothing has happened, yet.

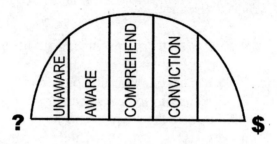

Stage #4: **Conviction**

Conviction is defined as:

"I understand what a product or service or idea can do FOR ME."

Without conviction, there is no commitment. Conviction is when your prospective teammate moves beyond rationally understanding what you are trying to do and says, "I want to be involved. Because of the benefits I see, what can I do? I understand, and I want to help make a difference."

Conviction is the ownership stage of commitment. It's when a person takes ownership of the process and makes it their own. Conviction wouldn't be so difficult, except you're working with two types of people:

Laggards and innovators.

Laggards don't want change. They don't want to attempt a higher level of living. They are content in their present state with no aspirations for anything better. They will whine and complain but never do anything about their circumstances. "It's the fault of the Chinese. It's fault of the Mexicans. It's the fault of the court system. The responsibility is with someone, but not me." Laggards adhere to the philosophy that there are only three types of people in the world:

> Those who are out to screw you and tell you before hand,
> Those that are out to screw you but don't tell you before hand,
>   and
> Those that are not out to screw you, but do so anyway.

Laggards would be harmless if that's where it ended, but they also
don't want anyone else to do any better either. If you do better, then
it shines a spotlight on their own poor choices in life. While you are
enjoying the panorama from a higher level of living, they are stuck
with the same dim view, the same low-level experience. And they
don't like that. They will say things like,

> "Why do you have to stir things up, cause this trouble?
> You're just fine where you are. Don't get so full of yourself
> with your ideas. Just do your work and shut up."

I had a friend who, several years ago, took a job at the U.S. Post
Office. He was a good worker. He had me record special music on
a cassette tape that he could listen to on his rounds that motivated
and energized him. He was so proficient at his tasks and so efficient
with his time that he could do three routes to everyone else's one.
Not that they couldn't do more, they choose not to. One day his co-
workers pulled him aside and said, "Stop it. You're making us look
bad. Just do your route and no more."

 I give him credit. He refused to give in to a low-level experience of
life. No matter what he did, he wanted to expand and grow,
personally and professionally, with or without the encouragement of
a laggard.

You will definitely being dealing with some laggards. How will you
respond?

Smile, thank them for their input and move on. Do not let them or
their words affect you in any way. The best thing they can do is get

out of your way. You have a life to live, and you will not give a
laggard permission to bring you down to his level.

I was fortunate to have been taught by an elderly gentleman to treat
criticism and praise exactly alike: listen to it for 2.3 seconds and then
move on. Take the kernel of truth in either, if it can make you better,
but forget the rest. Live your life according to your purpose and goal
(make sure you have one; review Step 2), and let the others live as
they choose.

Fortunately, there will be others who are innovators.
They like to see good change happen. They want to be
involved in making things better. Innovators will have
ideas to dovetail with yours. Use your innovators. Put
them to work. Let them do whatever they wish to
volunteer for. Your job in working with the innovator
is to remove barriers, supply resources, and get out of HIS way.
Innovators never have to be disciplined -- they will be harder on
themselves than you could ever be.

General Wesley K. Clark was at the Army's National Training
Center when he forwarded the "Socratic dialogue" form of teaching.
He would send observers out with every unit, with every
commanding officer. The idea was not to punish officers for their
mistakes nor to second-guess their decisions. The idea was not even
to hold officers **accountable** for their mistakes and decisions. The
idea was to encourage officers to hold *themselves* accountable. The
idea was to create a culture of accountability in which the Army's
enormous investment in training and education could take root and
flourish, and in which every soldier counted.

Yet, considering the vast caesium of difference between laggards and
innovators, both are moved from stage 3 comprehension to stage 4
conviction/ownership through the same three phases. Some may take
just one, others may take all three phases, it depends on the
individual.

Conviction/ownership is accomplished through:

Affiliation, Acknowledgment and Authority

- **Affiliation** is getting them involved in the process. Give them something to do, something that makes them feel included. We all feel the need to be affiliated with something or someone outside ourselves. It may be a church, a school, club or an association with common interests. The key is that everyone can feel the sense of belonging.

This revolutionary group must become theirs. They have to have a stake in its outcome and effectiveness. Saturn creates affiliation with their cars through customer picnics and birthday cards (to the car, no less!). They make you feel like you are part of a club rather than just buying pieces of metal, plastic and rubber.

Sports teams create affiliation by wearing uniforms that look alike. They eat together, go to meetings together, review films, exchange ideas together. They even complain about the coach together . . . but they're doing it together. Companies can do the same thing.

You can create affiliation by including members in a lunch or after-work meeting. Go bowling or eat Chinese, but do it together so you can swap stories and create that bond that only comes from shared experiences.

One of my clients flew his employees in from all over north America and their corporate office in Finland. The employees wanted to make a difference, but they didn't know how. So I invited a few of them from Chicago, Montreal, Vancouver and Texas to my house for a brainstorming session. We ate dinner on the patio table beside the pool, exchanged jokes and personal stories, and then moved into my living room where the conversation was relaxed, the ideas flowed, and a tremendous time was shared on how to have more success at what they were doing.

That's how you create affiliation.

- **Acknowledgment** is valuing the individual for the specific and unique contribution they make to the team. It's different than liking them, because on a personal level, you may not. They may or may not be your friend, but each person has a special talent they bring to a group dynamic. You must recognize that unique  contribution and capitalize on it. Use their abilities to make the group better. Their ideas may be couched in a personality style that irritates you, but find the golden kernel of truth and take full advantage of it. Soar with their strengths and manage their weaknesses. That's all any of us can do.

We each like the feeling of being appreciated. None of us wants to be ignored or taken for granted. Let others glow in the warmth of your appreciation for them as people and their role in your organization. With this acknowledgment, they will be moving towards a deeper level of commitment.

Acknowledgment can occur one-on-one individually or in a group setting, such as a staff meeting. Without embarrassing anyone, you can create an enormous bank of good-will when you publicly acknowledge the contribution and success stories of each other. When was the last time you received a round of applause? First grade Christmas pageant? Believe it or not, it'll make them feel the same way: appreciated and valued (without the shiny star on their head!)

I've had boards of directors give themselves a round of applause for all the complex work they accomplished and agreements they achieved in a short amount of time. I've had hardened foundry workers, gruff and brusque, stand up as a team and receive the applause of their co-workers for creative ideas that will advance their own revolution.

Lets, please, have a round of applause. And more of it.

*   **Authority** is giving someone permission to make a difference. Tell someone, "go ahead, make a choice, run with it." Call it empowerment or delegating or sanctioning, but authority is giving someone the permission to do it himself. So many people are afraid; afraid of screwing up, afraid of failing, afraid of succeeding, because they won't know what to do if it were to actually come true. Give them the authorization they already own within themselves, but have yet to express, to take that leap of faith and make something happen. As the little mouse had to ask himself in *Who Moved My Cheese*:

> **"What would you do if you weren't afraid?"**

There is a strong tendency in companies to isolate failure, to blame the culprit, and to not learn from mistakes. Organizations can do a lot to encourage their members to face up to failure, refuse to take shortcuts or simplify reality. There is an interesting story about the great German scientist Wernher non Braun. When a missile went out of control during pre-launch testing, von Braun sent a bottle of champagne to an engineer who confessed that he might have inadvertently short-circuited the missile. An investigation revealed that the engineer was right, which meant that expensive redesigns could be avoided.

You don't get a lot of admissions like that today. But all it takes is one such story to make an individual in the company stand up and take notice, "Hey, these folks are serious about facing up to failure, so I'm going to take my chances and speak up."

Action, tempered by reflection, is the critical component to giving authority.

Leap while looking!

Giving authorization is not condescending on your part, rather it is releasing the power that is already in them. You're giving permission to something they already possess. They just don't know it yet.

These three phases will move a laggard and an innovator from simply understanding what you are doing (comprehending) to owning the revolution for themselves (conviction). Once they have done that, stage five is readied.

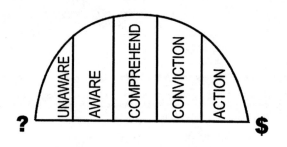

Stage #5: Action

Action is just what it says. Now what are you going to do? Action steps must be specific and direct. What do you want them to do? Come to a meeting. Invite a co-worker to join. Get a board member to tend the fund raising booth at the county fair. Call a bank and ask them to sponsor your event. Action steps cannot be vague or leave room for doubt or importance. Whatever you ask someone to do, make it directly connected to the purpose and goal of your revolution. What they do will make a difference.

These five stages must be experienced one stage at a time. For some, all five stages can be completed with one contact. For others, it takes time to progress from one stage to another. There is one exercise that will move people from stage to stage to stage. This one exercise is the foundation for all good selling, marketing and promotion. It's the caffeine in the coffee, the kick in codeine. It's:

Repetition

Repetition is the key to moving through all stages of commitment. We must continuously connect the objective of our activities directly to the desired goal. We must state at each meeting **why** we are doing what we're doing. Repetition is the key -- over and over again.

"But they'll get sick of it," you're saying. "If I say the same thing over and over again, they'll think I'm nuts and eventually not listen to me anymore."

Very true.

There is a fine line between being **persistent** and being a **pest**. You must understand the difference if you want to get others to join the revolution rather than dismiss it with, "been there-done that-heard it all before." Do you really want to be Herb Tarleck, radio salesman extrodinaire, from WKRP in Cincinnati? He is the epitome of the pesty salesman whom no one wishes to acknowledge. Just Run Away!

The answer to persistence is found in two phrases:

> **Always present *New* information**
> **while**
> **Varying the *modes* of communication.**

Imagine yourself snuggled nicely in your favorite lounger, early in the evening, a beverage in one hand, the remote in the other. The telephone rings. And rings again. Should you answer it or not? Oh, it could be your sister or your mother or your fishing buddy.

You better get up.

It rings again. Okay, okay. I'm coming. I'm coming.

 One more ring.

"Hello?"

"Good evening, Mr. Aksjdfrl (which is how badly they mangle your last name). I'd like to introduce you to our new lower rates for . . ." And with tremendous agitation, you slam the phone down in disgust, your evening interrupted by someone trying to sell you something you don't particularly want or especially need.

The telemarketer. Everyone's favorite pest. But why do we consider them a pest?

> Do we use the products they're selling (long distance service, credit cards, vacations)?

Yes! We use them all.

> Do we use the mode of communication for their pitch (the telephone)?

Yes...everyday.

> Do we take calls from other people in the evening or during a meal (a child, a relative a friend)?

Yes, of course we do.

So why are telemarketers perceived as being a pest when we use their products, utilize their mode of communication, and even take other calls at the same hour without the infuriating irritation?

Because we know what's coming before three words have escaped their mouths. We can anticipate the exchange before five seconds have passed. We have all been there and heard the script before.

The essence of persistence, then, is to provide NEW information while varying the MODES of communication. New information can be anything having to do with yourself, your group, your activities, your plans, your ideas, your training, your meetings, your statistics, anything and everything having to do with your revolution. Always have new information to share. If you say the same thing over and over again, of course people will get bored with you. Of course, they can't help but avoid you or make excuses why not to listen.

New information. New, New, New.

And then vary the modes of communication. Don't always send an e-mail. Leave a voice mail message. Create a brightly colored flier. Send a note. Create a newsletter. Make an announcement. Design a banner. Use your imagination to generate as many different WAYS to convey your message as you can.

Change your mode of communication and your new information every 30 to 90 days. If they see you coming, if they can anticipate what you're going to say before you open your mouth . . .you have become a pest -- someone worthy of ignoring.

Death to your revolution will be at your doorstep the moment you become a pest.

Instead, be persistent with new information and vary the modes of communication.

How to Get Anyone to Do Anything

One of the greatest challenges to your revolution is gaining the cooperation of those whom you seek help from to advance your goals. How do you get reluctant by-standers to give you what you need to continue moving forward? The answer is in how our minds work. When you understand how the human mind processes requests, you can better understand how to move people to help you -- even when they may not wish to. Follow the 4 steps in how to get anyone to do anything, and you won't have to get frustrated, angry or agitated.

I've used this system to get a request fulfilled with the telephone and cable company. I've gotten insurance companies to pay claim bills, medical clinics to give me doctor appointments, and kids to help around the house (it works with spouses, too, as long as they haven't read this book!). Just follow the steps in sequence and get more done.

Step 1: Limit their options. When you want someone to help you or supply something you need in order to complete your work, give him two, but no more than three options. Why do you even want to give someone a choice when you want them to do something?

For the same reason *you* would like a choice. We want to feel an element of self-determination in our lives, have a sense that, as adults, we can define the course of our lives. No one likes to be told what to do. So when you want someone to do something, always give him a choice. Either option is perfectly fine with you, just so he chooses one of the alternatives you offer.

Why only give two, no more than three options?

Because the mind can only handle so many choices before, at some point, freezing up in the evaluative process. We describe it as "deer caught in the headlights." You want a choice to be made from a limited selection, not offer the whole universe. Remember your first few steps into Disney World? You stood in awe, your head turning from side-to-side, wondering where should you begin. Where do you embark first with such an imposing array of choices? It's difficult to make up your mind, because you don't want to make the wrong choice and end up missing something you *really* wanted to do before your day runs out.

This is not Disney World. You have a revolution to attend to. Give them two, no more than three choices. Let them make their decision and move on. If you want a report, simply ask, "I could use your help. I need a copy of the budget report from last month. Would it be more convenient for you to fax it over, or can I stop by and pick it up?"

Two options. Easy choice.

If I wanted my son Trevor to wash the car this weekend, I would say, "Trevor, I'd like you to wash the car this weekend. Saturday or Sunday, doesn't matter to me. When would you like to do it?"

"Huh . . . Sunday?"

"You got it, Trev. Sunday it is."

Now, move to specific a time agreement.

Step 2: Work from a deadline. Nothing gets done unless there is an element of time. If you wanted the budget report from a co-worker and said, "give it to me as soon as you can," when would you receive it? A week, a month, a year later!

"I gave it to you as soon as I could!"

What if you said, "send it over when you can get around to it." Again, don't hold your breath. You need to have a specific time agreement, again with a choice, that will allow the other party to choose what, in his mind, is the best solution, yet accomplishes your intended purposes. Let's return to that budget report you need from a co-worker. He said he was pretty busy, could you stop over and pick it up? Not a problem.

"Would morning or afternoon work better for you? Say ten o'clock or two o'clock?"

"Oh, I'll have it copied and sitting here for you by ten."

"Fantastic. I'll be there at ten. I appreciate your help."

With my son washing the car I'd say, "We're going to use the car at five o'clock Sunday afternoon. Would you rather have the car washed by noon or three? Either one is fine with me."

"Huh . . . noon?"

"You got it. Sunday noon it is."

Now you have a specific time in which to gauge whether there is progress, completion or failure. Without time, without a deadline, you have nothing. You are at the mercy of the other party's assumption of what "as soon as you can" really means. This will not help you in accomplishing your goals.

Remember, the object is to complete a request. Not just work at it!

Step 3: Vocalize your expectations. It's important to say out loud what it is you have each agreed to do. Say it aloud. This is important, because our minds work differently in silence than out loud. In silent mode, one's mind does not need to process every word in order to understand the concept. When reading, we're not thinking about the "a's, the's, and's" and multitude of other letters and words. The mind glances over them, not needing to separately

analyze each element in order to comprehend the idea of each sentence.

For example, read the following paragraph:

> Aoccdrnig to a rscheearch at an Elingsh uinervtisy, it deosn't mttaer in waht oredr the ltteers in a wrod are, the olny iprmoetnt tihng is taht frist and lsat ltteer is at the rghit pclae. The rset can eb a toatl mses and you can sitll raed it wouthirt porbelm. Tihs is bcuseae we do not raed ervey lteter by itslef but the wrod as a wlohe.

You don't even need the letters in proper order! Your mind is capable of understanding what it's reading without processing each individual element.

This is why it's so important to say what your agreement will consist of out loud. The information is sent through a different filter in the mind, a filter that will pick up each element separately so nothing is misunderstood or forgotten.

After agreeing to stop by to pick up the report, you must say again, "I appreciate your help. I'll see you tomorrow at ten o'clock to pick up the copy of the budget."

After agreeing to wash the car by noon on Sunday, you say again, "That's great, Trevor. I appreciate your help. So I can count on the car being washed by noon on Sunday so we can use it by five. Is that correct?"

Repeating your agreements out loud helps ensure that everyone understands what is expected and both minds have the opportunity to pick up any inadvertent step that could be missed when agreeing silently, assuming the logistic details.

With your request affirmed and vocalized, you can now help him process the information in *his* mind.

Step 4: Help him process the information. Right now, I'd like you to think of something you do not like to do -- doesn't matter if its at home or work. What is it that you really don't like? Employee evaluations? Budget forecasting? Laundry? Grocery shopping?

When I asked you to think of something you do not like to do, your mind broke the task down into many, many steps, **none** of which you like, and any **one** of the steps is a perfectly good reason not to do it at all! Let's take grocery shopping. If you hate to grocery shop, your mind did the following:

✓ Ask everyone in the house what they want.
✓ Plan your meals for the next week.
✓ Combine your plan and their requests.
✓ Compare your plan and their requests with what you have in the cupboard.
✓ Make your list.
✓ When will you go: after work? on the weekend? when you have time?
✓ What store will you go to: best meat? freshest vegetables? convenience?
✓ Will you take the car or the van?
✓ Will you pay with check, cash, credit or debit card?
✓ Where do they stock the chocolate sprinkles you like so much?
✓ When did the price go up on cucumbers? Scratch them off the list.
✓ Wait in line for a checkout.
✓ Get ignored by the cashier who is talking to the bagger boy.
✓ Paper or plastic?
✓ Haul the groceries in the house, plop them on the counter, put them away.
✓ **Family complains there is no food in the house!**

Who would ever want to grocery shop again with this in mind?

Now, think of something you DO enjoy doing. Golfing? Swimming? Shopping with your grandchildren, niece or nephew? Your mind will not break down the process into multiple steps, but rather see the whole occasion as enjoyable. There isn't any consternation over who or where or what are you going to do. The whole operation is enjoyed and relished.

When you are asking someone to do something, more than likely it won't be his favorite thing to do. So, you must help him work through the steps necessary to complete it, so none of the steps are used as a reason for it not getting done.

When asking for a copy of the budget report, you'd ask, "Do you have it handy right there or is it electronically stored? Should I ask for you when I stop over, or will it be at the front desk with my name on it?" These questions will have to be answered in his own mind before he can fulfill your request, so ask him yourself in order to guide the process of completion within his own thoughts.

For Trevor (his mind racing, trying to think of a way to get out of this), I would say, "I know we need to get the hose down and connected to the spicket in back. Tell you what, I'll get the water hose and hook it up for you. You get the bucket, sponge and soap. After you have washed and rinsed the car, give me a call, and I'll help you shammy it dry." I'm helping him to process each step and see how it can be accomplished easily and efficiently.

Guide the other party through each point and assist him in any way you can to fulfill your request. Make it easy for him to say yes. Once you have confirmed the procedural activities, there is one question you must ask. Failure to ask this question at the end of your 4-step process may negate all your best efforts. After you have helped process the information and established the actions that will be required, ask:

Is there anything you need from ME to accomplish this?

The last thing in the world you want is for YOU to be the reason the job didn't get done. Always ask what is needed from you so that every last variable has been addressed. Without asking this question, you may show up at ten o'clock to pick up the budget report only to be queried, "Did you bring last month's sales figures for yourself? Because I only have mine included in this report. Sorry."

If it's five o'clock and the car is still dirty, I will track down my son and say, "I thought we had an agreement to have the car washed by noon?"

"Dad, who's gonna back it out of the garage. I'm only nine!"

Urggggggggg.&^%*#@(*!

Always ask, is there anything you need from me to accomplish this so YOU are never the excuse for something not getting finished as you expected. Use this 4-point system for getting anyone to do anything, and you'll discover more cooperation with your peers and managers and greater efficiency in completing your tasks and objectives.

Now you have attained commitment.

Now you're ready to charge ahead.

Now is a critical time, because you're moving towards actually getting something done.

Now you must remain organized and focused on the future.

Revolutionary Tactics to Increase Commitment

➡ To attain commitment, you must move a prospect through 5 stages:
    Unaware
    Aware
    Comprehend
    Conviction
    Action

➡ You will be dealing with both laggards and innovators. Learn to recognize each and their role in your revolution.

➡ For both laggards and innovators, commitment/ownership is accomplished through:
    Affiliation
    Acknowledgment
    Authority

➡ Use Repetition to move your prospective team through the 5 stages of the commitment cycle.

➡ Be persistent by:
    Always presenting new information, and
    Varying the modes of communication

➡ Gain greater cooperation by applying the techniques of getting anyone to do anything:
    Limit their options
    Work from a deadline
    Vocalize your expectations
    Help them process the information

➡ Always end the process by asking the critical question, "Is there anything you need from me to accomplish this?"

STEP 6 | **Stay Focused and Organized**
STEP 5 | Increase Commitment
STEP 4 | Manage The Change
STEP 3 | Build A Coalition
STEP 2 | Establish Your Goal
STEP 1 | Set Your Foundation

Step 6: Stay Focused and Organized

"The moment you wake up each morning, your wishes and hope for the day rush at you like wild animals. And the first job of each morning consists in shoving them all back; in listening to that other voice, taking that other point of view, letting that other, larger, stronger, quieter life come flowing in."

Every revolution has a time when the leadership tires or certain goals stagnate and begin to appear more and more allusive. Setbacks discourage the participants, and outright reluctance on the part of co-workers or management to participate create doubt as to whether you are really having any effect at all.

This is when you need to turn to Stan and Mabel.

I don't remember how I first met this couple. One spring day, a number of years ago, they just showed up in my backyard. I looked up from my work, glanced out the window, and there they were. They weren't disruptive or unruly, just a bit too comfortable using someone's backyard without the owner's permission. I was a bit taken back to just run out and say, "Hey! What do you think you're doing?" So I would leave them alone, and they would sun themselves for a few hours, take a dip in the pool, and then just disappear until the next day.

Over the years, I discovered they only lingered through the months of May and June, popping in and out, resting from their travels, as I deduced they lived in the south for the winter. Just your typical, garden-variety couple of snow birds, coming and going as they please, only without an RV parked in the driveway and a yipping Schitsu pacing the front seat.

You see, Stan and Mabel are two ducks . . . mallards to be exact.

Stan and Mabel (my personal names for them) come to my backyard pool to swim, wash themselves, get a drink, rest and relax from their journey . . . just these two, and no others (apparently the other ducks found accommodations more luxurious than my humble backyard pond). I can watch Stan and Mabel from my home office window as they warm themselves in the early summer sunshine. With an approaching storm developing, I was soon to observe a lesson on how to stay focused in the midst of swirling circumstances, and I literally mean swirling!

I could see the wind picking up very quickly, and I watched Stan and Mabel to see how long they were going to hang around. I expected them to pack up and fly off at any minute, going wherever ducks go when there is a storm. For the moment, they were sitting on the patio deck, feet tucked up underneath themselves, facing south.

As the winds pick up intensity, their feathers began to ruffle. Again, I expected them to fly away at any minute. But instead, they made a slight turn to the west so they would be facing the oncoming wind. As the gusts continued to increase, with stronger and stronger velocity, Stan and Mabel adjusted and turned themselves until they were directly facing west, confronting the storm head-on.

When branches started to fling off the trees and the howling wind turned into a full-fledged gale, Stan and Mabel calmly slipped into the water, just off the edge of the pool, continuing to face the storm, serenely wading in the water, holding their position, not panicking in any way.

The storm quickly raged through, rain, wind, branches flying everywhere and, yet, the ducks bobbed up and down as if on some mildly-amusing carnival joy-ride. When the winds died down, the sun peeking out from behind the clouds, Stan and Mabel hopped out of the pool, shook the raindrops from their back, sat down and, once again, resumed their original pre-storm position.

It was an amazing sequence of unexpected actions -- these two ducks knowing perfectly well how to handle themselves, and what I think is a wonderful model of what to do when storms of resistance blow our way.

❖ *Do not run away (or fly away for that matter)!* At the first hint of trouble, the ducks did not take off as I thought they would. They stayed right where they were until they had more information as to what was coming. We, too, need to "stay the course." Too often, at hearing one discouraging word from a co-worker or receiving one disparaging look from a resistant manager, we run, hide, stop whatever it is we're doing, without knowing if there is any real or on-going danger at all.

Wait.

Pause.

Then continue with your work. That may be all there is to it.

B) *Make small adjustments.* When the intensity of the storm increased, Stan and Mabel very simply adjusted their course with barely a trace of movement. They conformed to the best position for survival, turning ever so slightly, until facing it head on.

We, too, need to make small adjustments, very small adjustments during this time. Making broad, sweeping changes only creates more turbulence. Some people, when losing their jobs (as if that weren't disrupting enough) add uncertainty by moving to a different city or going to excess with unhealthy behavior in drinking or drugs. They swing the pendulum so far opposite of where they were, it becomes more difficult than necessary to return to a healthy state of life.

If only they had made small adjustments that simply put them in a better position for when the storm passed. Instead of moving to a new city, they could have taken a few classes that would have broadened their skill level. Instead of excessive, destructive behavior, they could have taken regular walks or talked to their family a little more. These small adjustments could have carried them through the assault.

* *When at its worse, move to safe surroundings.* When the going gets really rough, the storm is at its peak, you don't know how much worse it can get, do the duck thing. Stan and Mabel quietly slipped into safe, more familiar surroundings. They moved into their natural environment, the water. There, they knew how to handle the storm, what actions to take underneath the water to maintain their position. They were confident in how to ride it out.

When the discouragements get tough, and you're not sure if you're doing the right thing, move quietly into a safer environment. Rather than take another beating, talk to friends who know, respect and support your efforts. Reaffirm your values and the rationalizations for why you aspire to accomplish your goals. Reacquaint yourself with the familiar and protected ground of co-workers who will back you up and remind you of the good results that have already been achieved. Dr. Martin Luther King taught us:

> *"The measure of a man is never perfection,*
> *but what he does upon reflection."*

Storms DON'T last forever . . . although, at times, that's how it seems. We can't quite see the sun -- but it's there, and it will show itself again. Follow the example of Stan and Mabel: Don't run away, but rather look around, evaluate the circumstances and your position, before you do anything. Don't make big changes; instead, make small adjustments in order to face the storm head-on. In the midst of its greatest intensity, quietly move into a safe environment where you reaffirm your values and "bob" with the temporary waves, until that time when the storm passes and you are able to re-establish your activities and enjoy the sunshine.

Resolving Conflict Between Departments

Storms come in a variety of forms and situations wherever you have people working together. When departments are not cooperating with each other, internal conflict is the norm, people aren't talking, and there's a contentious, competitive atmosphere, you have the makings of a disaster.

"I'm not helping them. They didn't help me when I needed it."

"I hope they screw up and get fired. Then maybe they'll hire my friend."

"I had to learn the hard way. So should you."

"After 35 years, I'm not changing how I do things. Leave me alone."

I have used and taught the **Five Rules to Resolution** whenever people are not getting along. The five rules work in professional, as well as personal, areas of conflict, because it's based on dissension between humans, no matter where they happen to be. The Five Rules to Resolution provide a *system* for creating real solutions. How often have you heard, "Why can't you just get along? Let's have a meeting and talk about this. You need to communicate more."

Do any of these work? Do any of these provide a foundation for a workable resolution so you're not having the same conversations over and over again? No. In order to produce real solutions, a system is needed to guide the conversations toward workable, realistic solutions. Otherwise, we're just going in circles about personalities and age-old grudge matches.

The Five Rules To Resolution

Rule Number One: Identify the common goal. You have to have SOMETHING in common if you are going to reach any agreement. The commonality may be just keeping your jobs. Maybe it's not to get into any more trouble with your boss. Maybe it's just to be able to function together in order to get your jobs done. But there must be a common goal you both wish to satisfy. Without a common goal, there is no reason to form agreements of any kind. And certainly no reason to abide by them if you happen to casually agree to something anyway. So identify what it is you both wish to accomplish in the realm of your daily living.

Let's say the accounting department and the shop manager are not getting along very well. There has been disagreement about when the time cards ought to be turned in for payroll. As they sit down to meet, they could agree to the common goal that everyone gets paid on time. The accountant wants to get his work done on time, as that is his job, and the shop manager wants his people paid on time.

Rule Number Two: Identify what's missing for smooth operation. The facts, not the personalities. This is the most dangerous part of most disagreements. We use personalities as the battle field of engagement. This is not the time to be talking about how "Bob has done it that way for 50 years. He'll never change." Or, "That's Mary. She's always late." "What's missing for a smooth operation" must be described as a set of facts. This is not about who, but about what.

The three most common causes of conflict will be found in the Process, the Communication or the Priorities. Process conflicts arise when there are no clearly defined or described activities. "A" doesn't get to "B" which, in turn, disrupts the work of "C."

Communication conflicts occur when information is not fully transferred to all parties involved. The information may not have been entirely transferred by the sender, some piece was missing. Or the information was not fully understood by the receiver, or the information was misinterpreted by both.

Priority conflicts are apparent when one party has an idea of what should be done first, while another has a differing viewpoint. Neither is right or wrong, just different perspectives on what should be achieved first in relation to the goal.

What's missing for these people or these departments to function well together, process, communication, priorities or a combination of all of them? In our example, the shop manager's job is to get the payroll hours to the accounting department by 12 noon on Friday in order for checks to be cut by three o'clock. If the checks are not being cut on time, the accounting department would describe the facts in terms of process by saying, "The payroll hours don't arrive until two o'clock."

These are the facts. Not "Pete never gets the hours here like he should. He's always in a hurry to get to his bowling league." The *who* doesn't matter. What matters is getting the payroll hours to a certain place by a certain time in order to accomplish the common goal that everyone be paid on Friday before they leave work at three o'clock.

Rule Number Three: Identify the PHYSICAL action steps to resolve #2. Notice how I emphasize the word "physical." That's because the goal of finding a real solution is to determine what physically has to be accomplished to solve what's missing from a smooth operation. We are not looking for a change in personality. We are not looking for someone to get a better attitude. We are looking for the physical activities needed so this conflict can be resolved for good.

Again, steering clear of the personalities, the accountant could say, "What I need is the total payroll hours faxed to me by noon each Friday." The shop manager might say, "In order to do that, I have to make sure everyone's hours are completed by 11:00 a.m. to give me enough time to collate and send them off by noon. But it gets real busy around that time on Friday. Could you give a quick reminder call about 10:30, and that'll help me finish up what I'm doing in order to collect the workers hours?"

Every real and workable resolution is accomplished with a physical activity. For people and departments to function together in harmony, we must establish PHYSICAL action steps that can be delivered **regardless** of attitude, personality traits or how someone feels that day. Always couch your solutions to any disagreement within the sphere of the physical movements needed to supply what's missing. THEN you'll have the start to real agreements rather than trying to change someone's attitude.

Rule Number Four: Identify the benefits to each side for doing #3.

There must be benefits to both sides for agreeing to do what they are going to do. Agreements must always have a balance of benefit. In my mediation work for family court, if two adults come to surface agreements, yet, one party feels like he gave in a little more or compromised a little father than the other, how long will that agreement last? Not long -- maybe a step or two out the door. That's why there must be a balance of benefit for both sides to do what they've agreed to do.

If the accountant stops his work and makes a reminder call at 10:30, she will have increased the odds that the shop manger will send the payroll hours before noon. Her job can then get done. If the shop manager gets the payroll hours in before noon, he is assured of payroll checks by three in order to hand out to his workers before they leave for the weekend. He's a hero!

Everyone wins.

But even then, there must be something that motivates people to do what they've agreed to do, especially when they don't feel like it. Which brings us to rule number five.

Rule Number Five: Identify the accountability system to adjust and adapt. Nothing is ever perfect the first time. There must always be

adjustments to every agreement once you've put it into practice. What happens, all too often, is as soon as something goes wrong, one party says, "See, I told you this wouldn't work," then throws the whole agreement out the window, and blames it on the personality.

What must be done with ALL agreements is to build in an accountability system to adjust and adapt . . .making sure all parties do what they agreed to do, even when they don't feel like it. This system could be in the form of a piece of paper that is signed or initialed and turned in. It could be a manager's evaluation once a month to check on the process. Or make this topic a subject of each Monday morning staff meeting; are the payroll hours getting to the accounting office by noon each Friday?

Maybe the shop manager notes the time payroll hours are sent right on the payroll sheet itself to indicate that he met his agreed upon time objective. The accounting department could circle the time printed on the fax, allowing the department manager to see that it was received on time.

There will always be moments when we don't feel like doing what we've agreed to do. We get rushed, we get busy, or we just don't feel like it.

When I was speaking to groups of doctors in Kansas on how to increase patient satisfaction, I was driving from one end of the state to the other. Did you know you can set your cruise control in Topeka, head west and not touch it again for six hours? The state of Kansas has an effective accountability system that helped me to adjust and adapt even when I didn't feel like following the rules when driving through their state. It included contributing to the Kansas State Trooper fund-- which I did THREE TIMES–to the tune of $176.00 each time. I did learn eventually (the last ticket was within two miles of the airport for my return flight home). I was just a little slower than most. A simple accountability system helps everyone to follow what we've agreed to do, even when we don't feel like it.

The Five Rules to Resolution are terrific for preventative maintenance, as well. Why wait for something to go wrong? Once a month, choose two departments, and go through the five rules to identify what may be missing for everything to be running a little more effortlessly. What physical action steps need to be established to ensure the wheels never fall off our operation? What are the benefits to each side, and what accountability measures will be put in place to ensure that everything is being done at its proper time and place? Follow this system, and you'll find REAL resolutions rather than saying, "Didn't we talk about this before? "

Internal Customers

We each have internal customers who receive the output of our work. At times, we are the internal customer, while another department is our supplier. Where do you begin your resolution process if there is departmental conflict up and down the line? We all are dependent on each other. How are we ALL going to be able to get our work done?

When we don't receive what we need, our first reaction is to point fingers -- blame someone else for our problem. We are the internal customers of each other. Rather than play the blame game, you are now going to take a proactive approach and start your own revolution of successful resolution.

First, go back one department and apply the five rules to resolution. If you are talking to people of your same rank and position, your peers, then you can go one-on-one. Have a conversation with them, and go through the five rules. Identify your common goal, what's missing and what could be done to resolve it to everyone's benefit. If they refuse to engage in this conversation, then you may need to involve a higher supervisor in the process in order to go through the five rules.

If your dispute is with a supervisor or someone with a higher position than yours, never go alone, never talk one-on-one. Take two or three of your co-workers to engage in this type of dialogue. The reason is that one-on-one, you will always be "outnumbered" with a manager. Power is on the side of title. With more people than yourself, you have witnesses to agreements (accountability system), and it creates peer pressure, even with your boss.

Getting It Done

Staying focused and organized also means making the best use of your time. You have but one life, and you wish to make a difference. Then your time is your most valuable asset -- how are you going to use it? There are certain traps that steal our time, take it away, never to be recovered. Once stolen, you can only say you will do things differently in the future.

The three most common time traps are: Procrastination, Perfectionism and Carelessness (a lack of Priority setting).

Procrastination. What can you do when you have a hard time getting started on projects we dread: employee evaluations, budgets, cleaning out the garage? Or we look at projects that are so BIG, so overwhelming, that we don't know where to begin. Maybe it so complex, we feel that any 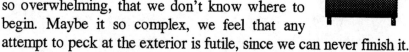 attempt to peck at the exterior is futile, since we can never finish it.

So, we set our minds with grim determination, resolving that this Thursday afternoon, I will shut my door, I will take the phone off the hook, I will dig in and really get a chunk of this project done. About a half hour into it, we stretch, get up, walk around, refill our coffee, and, as long as we're up, it'll take just a minute to check my e-mail, say hi to Bob (haven't talked to him all day) and, soon, an unproductive hour has slipped away. So we resolve that Friday will be our day to dig in (oops, full schedule already planned). Alright, then Monday. Yep, Monday will be the day . . . .

We put off and put off and put off. The answer to procrastination is the same answer to the old riddle, "How do you eat an elephant?" One bite at a time.

The answer to procrastination is a technique that, when applied, will radically change how much you actually get done. It's called

"Take 15"

With any project you are having a hard time getting started on, make an agreement with yourself to work on it for 15 minutes . . . no more. Just 15 minutes. Because we all have 15 minutes. We can work on it before lunch or prior to going home. We can even take 15 minutes when we're tired because, after all, its only 15 minutes.

When we make an agreement with ourselves to work on something for 15 minutes and no more, a number of wonderful things can happen:

> We work on it for MORE than 15 minutes. The time slipped away to 30 minutes, 45 or more.

> We might see a door open up to reveal the next logical step to progress.

> It wasn't as bad as we first thought. Still would rather do something else, but it's not all horrible.

You can feel good that you completed 15 minutes; it was an attainable goal.

You're building momentum.

And most important, if you worked on it for just 15 minutes and that's all, when the time was up, you put it away and were done with it, are you 15 minutes ahead of where you were yesterday? Yes. And if you "Take 15" tomorrow, will you be 30 minutes ahead of where you were 2 days ago? Yes. And if you "Take 15" once a day, by the end of the week, you will be an hour and a half or two hours into a project that, not long ago, you couldn't even get started.

You'll be amazed at what you begin to accomplish when you Take 15.

Perfectionism.   How many of you would rather do something yourself because it would get done faster and be done right the first time anyway? We don't want to relinquish a task or project, because we want it to be perfect. Our own good intentions get in the way of actually accomplishing something. We want it to be good. We want it to be perfect. Our name and reputation are on it! The answer to this time trap, this stealer of your most important asset, is simple and yet profound.

Let it go.

Let it go. We, perfectionists, must train ourselves to let it go. And I said "train ourselves ," because we will NEVER FEEL LIKE IT. It must be a conscience decision based on a rational sequence of logic. Follow me:

Is there anyone perfect in this world? Are you perfect? Am I perfect? The answer is no.

Is this a perfect world? Is there any way to attain perfection in this present life? No.

If I am not perfect within an imperfect world, can I ever produce perfect work within myself? No again. It's metaphysically impossible.

THEREFORE, the paradox is that something cannot get better, or become closer to perfection, until we let it go. Let the processes of life, the interaction with other points of view (remember the Armillary Sphere) allow your work to become better and better. But, something can't get better unless you let it go.

A quadraplegic artist in New York City once said,

"It's always wrong before it's right."

This is true of everything. There is nothing we have done that was perfect the first time. So let it go. It will always be wrong before it's right.

When I was learning how to write ads for the radio, I was taught a valuable lesson by my mentor. He asked, "What is the purpose of a commercial? What are we trying to achieve when someone hears an ad?" The answer is: a response. We want a response from the listener. We want him to respond in some way. Pick up a telephone, give us a call, stop by and take a look, hopefully buy something. But, it all begins with a response.

He then gave his maxim for writing successful radio ads by announcing,

"An imperfect ad on the radio will get more response than the perfect one sitting in your typewriter."

As copy writers, we might struggle to find the perfect word, that just-right phrase that will wow, excite and compel the listener to stop whatever it is he is doing and follow our directive. But, with every minute that passes, while we try to attain perfectionism, the listener is listening to someone else . . . someone who is actually on the air and inviting his response.

So, let it go. Your project, your task, will be just fine after you have done your best. Now let it go and move on. You will get more done and the world will be better for your contribution.

I am not talking about mediocrity or sloppiness or laziness. As perfectionists, those words have no meaning to us. Our standard is already a notch or two higher, so let it go. It'll already be better than most and, more importantly, you will have put it into practice. It will only get better from here.

Carelessness (lack of Priority setting). Carelessness of our time is one of the most insidious thieves. We don't even know our time is gone when we carelessly let it go. We have confused activities with accomplishments. We think that being "busy" is the same as getting something meaningful done. Setting priorities is imperative if you really want to get things done. Here is an effective, three-grade system that will guide you to doing the right things at the right time.

Did you catch that? Did I say, this will help you to get EVERYTHING done? Can you get everything done you want to get done in any given day? No. Time management is NOT about getting everything done -- it's impossible. Effective time management is:

> **Getting the right things done
> at the right time.**

How do I know I'm getting the right things done, the most important things? Everything on my "to do" list is important -- I think.

Give your "to do" list this simple three-grade system, and you will ensure you are doing the right things at the right time. It's as simple as A,B,C.

With every activity, give it a grade of A, B or C.
> A = Activities that are important AND urgent
> B = Activities that are important but NOT urgent
> C = Activities that are neither important nor urgent

But Everything is an "A"! It's all due right now!

Apply this acid test to determine if an activity is really an "A" level activity or not. Ask,

> "Are there any negative consequences if I don't do it RIGHT NOW?"

If the answer is no, then you have an automatic "B" -- it's important, but it can wait until this afternoon or tomorrow or a later time. If the answer is yes, there will be negative consequences if I don't do it right now, then it truly is an "A."

What defines "right now?" That's up to you. You can say it each hour if need be: "Are there negative consequences if I don't do it within this next hour?" Or you can say "right now" is this morning or this afternoon. "Are there any negative consequences if I don't do it this morning?" Keep it to a 1- 4 hour time window, so you stay focused to a specific time period.

This question will help you determine what you should be doing right now to accomplish the important things of life.

And if you always do your "A's" first, everything else will fall into place. You are no longer trying to do everything . . . instead, you're accomplishing the right things...the important things at the right time. Once you begin to do your A's first, you'll be amazed at how much time opens up to do your B's and C's.

The problem with level B and C activities is they are fun or enjoyable or easy. We are distracted by them, they lure us away with "you deserve a break," or "this won't take much time at all." I'm not saying that you shouldn't do your B or C activities. Just do them AT THE RIGHT TIME.

Just try saying to yourself, "I vow not to do any C's today. They WILL NOT distract me." That's like saying, "I'm never going to eat chocolate again. Never." As soon as you say that, what will you crave obsessively for the next 24 hours? Or 24 days! Chocolate! It'll be on your mind no matter how hard you fight and fight the urge.

The same is true of our B and C activities. When we vow not to do them or allow them to distract us, we obsess, we can't help but think about them. The object is not about NOT doing them. In fact, go ahead . . . **when your A's are done!** Once the A's are done, go ahead. DO a B or C level activities. Have fun...guilt-free fun, because you have accomplished what was important and urgent **first.**

Carelessness of time is resolved with consistent priority setting. Set your A's, do them, and your life will be better tomorrow than it was today.

2 Tips About Your "To Do" List

#1 Once you have made your "to do" list and prioritized it according to A, B and C level activities, read your list out loud.

Remember step #3 in "How to get anyone to do anything" -- vocalize your expectations? The same is true in this scenario. When you read something out loud, your brain sends the information through another filter, a different filter, than when we read silently. When you read silently, your mind does not process every word; it doesn't have to in order to understand the concept. So, our mind skips over what could be important information concerning our "to do" list.

Read your list out loud ,and I guarantee that, at some point as you say out loud each item on your list, you will snap your fingers and go, "Oh, yeah . . . that's right. I forgot about . . ." By reading it out loud, your mind will have sent the information through another filter, and it will remember something it didn't previously, reading the list silently to yourself. Give it try. You'll be surprised at what you remember.

#2 How do you keep from being interrupted? You've set your priorities, you know exactly what you're going to accomplish, when it'll be done and what is to come next. But within three minutes of starting, the telephone is ringing, someone wants a report, others are asking your opinion, your boss dumps five more projects on your plate, and soon your entire day is spent running around, putting out fires like a madman. You are so tired and worn out by the end of the day, you say, "I was SOOOOOO busy today, but I didn't get a thing . . . done."

Have you ever felt this way? We all have. After just such a day, my office manager, Lisa, came in, sat down and in tears said, "I can't take it anymore. Everyone want's something from me! I can't get a thing done."

It was then I taught her a skill that has helped me stay on track and not allow the interruptions of the day to steal my time. This is how to stay in control of your day and get more done. It's called

Living Inside - Out

Imagine this circle is your perfectly planned day. Each activity has been scheduled and you know exactly what you're working on and when it will be done.

But within three minutes, someone crashes in and says, "I need this now." Or the phone is ringing with someone else's demands, and each arrow pierces into your life and your perfect plan. Soon you are running around taking care of everyone else's projects and problems.

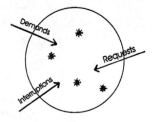

Now imagine that this circle represents a submarine. If you were to take that submarine down into the depths of the ocean and pierce its sides, what would happen? It would cave in, implode on itself. The pressure from the outside would collapse the inside. Isn't that the way we feel some days? Everyone has pierced our perfectly planned day, and we end up feeling crushed by the pressure outside ourselves. We didn't get a thing done.

You and I need to create equalized internal pressure. Just like the submarine needs equalized internal air pressure in order to control and resist the outside pressure, so we, too, need to create equalized internal pressure to keep everyone from imploding our day and our lives. We create this equalized internal pressure with two questions.

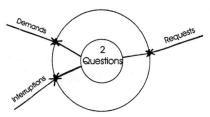

When someone comes into your life, rather than letting them automatically pierce your day with their demands, you meet them with two questions. Question number 1:

Am I the right person to be handling this request?

In other words, are you REALLY the best person, or can someone else handle this? If it's a payroll question, send them to payroll. If it involves someone else who can answer the question just as easily, then delegate it.

But some of you say "yes" to everyone. That's called the "Savior complex." You like to ride in on the white horse and rescue everyone, answering all questions and solving all problems. If that describes you, then there are other, deeper issues to come to grips with. This type of behavior is only destructive to you, as everyone else is getting their questions answered and work completed. You, meanwhile, are languishing with uncompleted "A" activities that are quickly reaching a crisis point.

But if you can honestly say, "No, I am not the right person to be handling this, go see Bob in payroll. He can answer your question." Or "See Mary in Purchasing. She has a better and more accurate answer than I can give you," then you will have created equalized internal pressure, and you have remained in control.

The first question to ask is: Am I the right person to be handling this request?

However, what if the answer is Yes -- you are the right person. This really does fall within your area of responsibility. Then you create equalized internal pressure with the second question:

> ## *"Is this the right TIME to be handling this?"*

I would bet that 99 times out of a 100 you can answer with, "I am the right person, but this is NOT the right time." You might say, "You're right, I am the right person, but right now I'm working on _____. Can I see you this afternoon about 2, and we'll talk about it then?" Or you might say, "You're right, I am the right person, but right now I'm working on _____. I'll be done in an hour. I'll come and see you then." You could even say, "You're right. I am the right person. Right now I'm working on _____. If you can wait just 10 minutes, quietly, over in that chair, then I can help you."

IF they can't wait 10 minutes while you complete your "A" level activity, was it really that important to them or that disastrous of an emergency? No, but you have stayed in control. You created equalized internal pressure to keep the sides of your life from collapsing.

If the answer to both question is "yes," you are the right person and there will be negative consequences if you don't handle it right now, then you have a TRUE emergency. You will have to handle it as efficiently as possible and get back to your "A" activity.

But the vast majority of time, you can say, "Now is not the right time,"and schedule when that right time is in order to get your priority tasks done first. When you create equalized internal pressure, you are staying in control. You are staying focused. You are not allowing outside forces to implode your day. You are living Inside-Out.

The next day, I came into work and looked to my left where Lisa's door is always open. That's how Lisa is. Everyone comes to her, because she usually does have the right answer anyway. But after teaching her to live Inside-Out, I saw that her door was closed. I was curious, so I walked over and saw a sign hanging from the door handle, probably absconded from some local hotel, because it read

"DO NOT DISTURB."

So, like any good boss, what did I have to do? Walk in!

"Lisa, this is great! You're taking control. You're living Inside-Out!" And without hesitation, pointing toward the door she replied, "**Now** is not the time!"

Living Inside-Out, Lisa had learned that everything has a time and place, even good and proper things. She had determined that the first hour of the day, from 7:30-8:30 a.m., was her time to get the logs ready for the announcers and the proposals ready for the salespeople. At 8:30 a.m., her door opened wide, and how do you think everyone else's day went after that? Smooth as glass. Lisa had said to herself, "I am the right person, but NOW is not the right time."

Begin to create equalized internal pressure by living Inside-Out. Honestly ask yourself, "Am I really the right person to be handling this?" and "Is now the right time?" You'll find yourself with calmer days and, most importantly, you'll be getting your "A" level activities done and on time.

Remember, you're not trying to get EVERYTHING done in your day, just the right things done at the right time!

With your successes building one on top of another, you'll begin to see yourself making real progress. Soon you will want to pass the baton to others, show them the skills you have learned, so your circle of influence can expand and grow farther than you ever imagined.

Revolutionary Tactics to
Stay Focused and Organized

➡ When storms approach, do not run away. Instead, make small adjustments and move to safer surroundings.

➡ To resolve interdepartmental conflict, apply the Five Rules to Resolution:
>   Identify the common objective
>   Identify what's missing for a smooth operation
>   Identify the physical action steps
>   Identify the benefits for both parties
>   Identify the accountability system to adjust and adapt

➡ Recognize the 3 most common areas of conflict:
>   The process
>   The communication
>   The priorities

➡ Avoid the 3 most common Time Traps:
>   Procrastination: apply "Take 15"
>   Perfectionism: train yourself to let it go
>   Carelessness: always set priorities – do your "A" level
>   activities first

➡ Make your "to do" list more effective by:
>   Reading your list out loud
>   Beginning to live Inside/Out to manage interruptions

STEP 7 | Pass the Baton
STEP 6 | Stay Focused and Organized
STEP 5 | Increase Commitment
STEP 4 | Manage The Change
STEP 3 | Build A Coalition
STEP 2 | Establish Your Goal
STEP 1 | Set Your Foundation

Step 7: Pass the Baton

*"As you live your life from this moment to next
Please think about those whose paths you cross.
Even if they stand right in front of you,
Take one little step that can – And will,
Make all the difference, in the world."*

In track and field competition, I've always been amazed by the relay race. The first member of the team will launch off the starting blocks with the baton firmly held in hand. If that were me, I'd be hanging on so tight, not to drop the dumb thing, embarrassing myself and losing the race, you'd have to pry the baton out of my fingers with a jaws of life. Yet, these racers will sprint around the track and, without breaking stride, sync their steps to the second teammate, running in tandem, reach out, let go and pass the baton. That racer will suddenly burst ahead, baton firmly in his care and take off around the track, only to do the same with the next teammate and the next.

They never look at each other. They KNOW where the other person is to be. They FEEL each other's presence, the outstretched baton. All the racer has to do is look straight ahead, run with arm stretched back, palm open and accept the gift. Once in a while there is a drop, but with some additional practice and technique refinement, they're running the race again, this time without a hitch.

The same is true of your revolution and all the positive changes you're going to make. There comes a time when you need to pass the baton. You can't do it all by yourself. This is not a one-person life. It requires the help of everyone who will be involved with you, who will contribute and add to the progressive outcome.

The Bridge Builder

An old man going a lone highway,
Came at the evening, cold and gray,
To a chasm, vast and deep and wide
Through which was flowing a sullen tide.
The old man crossed in the twilight dim,
The sullen stream had no fears for him,
But he turned when safe on the other side,
And built a bridge to span the tide.

"Old Man," said a fellow pilgrim near,
"You are wasting your time with building here,
You never again will pass this way,
Your journey will end with the closing day.
You have crossed the chasm, deep and wide,
Why build you this bridge at evening tide?"
"Good friend, in the way I've come," he said,
"There followed after me today
A youth whose feet must pass this way.
This stream that has been as naught to me,
To the fair-haired youth might a pitfall be.
He, too, must cross in the twilight dim,
Good friend, I am building a bridge for him."   – Author Unknown

How do you pass the baton?

What are the best techniques for transferring the principles and values of your revolution from one person to the next?

Who do you pass the baton to first?

As indicated in Step 4, you should choose an innovator to begin the process, someone who also wishes to see good change happen and is willing to do his part. Just as in the relay race, it is passed one person at a time. You may, at times, speak to groups of people, whether in your department or at a board meeting, but it's still the personal, one-on-one contact that will have the greatest impact. Once you have the first person on board, you move on to another, then another, and another. In the mean time, you're asking your first innovators if they know someone who is thinking like you do, others in their own sphere of influence that would like to join in and make a revolution ensue. Invite them to participate, as well. You will eventually form a group, a gathering, a critical mass, but it all begins with one.

Your most effective teams will be 12 or less. More than 12, and you may have factions that can split and weaken your efforts, sometimes without you even knowing it. If one or two people are creating dissension, there will be 10 others to apply peer pressure. Peer pressure is something we were taught to avoid in junior high school. But, as adults, peer pressure is an effective tool to maintain group cohesiveness and bring all thoughts and ideas into a single, powerful force.

Here are several leadership quick keys to convey the message that the contributions of each individual is valuable and appreciated for the success of the team. The theme of this book is not leadership, yet, the thought process and applications are the same. Apply these techniques of successful leaders, and you will find your revolution with more volunteers than you imagined.

Leadership Quick Keys

Say "Yes . . . and"

Say "Yes . . . and" rather than "Yes . . . but." When we say the word "and," we are implying that everything before "and" and everything after "and" is equal and can co-exist in the same discussion. When someone brings up a thought, you can respond with

> "Yes...I can see your point. Let's add it to the list. And I think there may be other alternatives, as well. Who else has an idea?"

"And" allows the thoughts of others to be part of the discussion without demeaning or humiliating their ideas. When we say "but," the message we are really conveying is that whatever was said before didn't really matter, because what you are about to say is what counts.

> "Yes...we could do what you suggest. BUT what if it doesn't work? Then what are we going to do? et's look at a different idea."

But" says that my thoughts are more important than your thoughts. "I know you say it was an accident, but...were you really paying attention?" "But" says I don't believe you. You will be more effective at engaging meaningful conversations with explosive new ideas when you begin to say "Yes...and."

Ask "What if ..."

Ask "What if ..." rather than demanding. No one likes to be told what to do. No matter our age, young or not so young, we naturally shrink back from being demanded to perform. We like to have a say in what affects and involves our lives. Rather than demanding people do what you want done, ask, "What if ...."

By asking "what if," you are communicating the sincere intention that you want input and participation. You are building options without commitments, alternatives without criticism. This is so important if you are to build what Roger Fisher calls in *Getting to Yes*, the ZOPA, the zone of possible agreement. The more alternatives you can include in your discussion, the more apt you will be to formulate the best choices. Rather than telling someone what you think is best, simply ask, "what if...." This allows your thoughts to be included in the discussion without demanding people do only what you think is best to do.

Ask, "what would it take to..."

Ask, "what would it take to..." rather than "don't screw up again." Every event in life offers a choice: we can look ahead to a better future, or look behind at a past we cannot change. Future vision is the positive choice, because it creates an opportunity to make a difference. When people don't do what we envisioned, or the outcome does not meet our expectations, we are always advancing a more constructive future by asking, "what would it take to..." and look ahead for what physical action steps are needed to make a positive change.

> There is no such thing as failure, only results.
> If you don't like the result you're getting, change something and get a different result.

The only functional effect of looking in the past is to identify a mis-step so corrective action can be implemented next time around. By asking, "what would it take to...," we are slipping past any possible personality differences and into real physical changes to make a more productive future.

What we allow - We teach

What we allow -- We teach. This one phrase has the potential for more impact on your revolution than anything else you will do. What we allow -- we teach is a powerful avenue to affirm the values and principles that serve as the bedrock of your aspirations. We are first and foremost teachers. We just don't realize it.

When a co-worker shuffles in, complaining about the boss or about his job, and you listen without a word, what you have taught him? That his behavior is okay. It's okay to complain, and it's okay to complain to you. You have just established a norm.

When a manager bursts into your office and demands, "This is the new priority -- I need it done right now,"and you don't say a word, instead, you nod your head and, with grim determination, put aside everything you were working on that is due in two hours and plow into this new project, what have you just taught your manager? That it's okay to dump on you without discussion or consideration for your priorities or projects.

What we allow -- we teach. Whatever passes through your day without comment or interjection, you've just taught, that's okay. I want to make a crystal clear statement, however; this does not give you permission to be a jerk or demeaning or defensive. Not at all! Just because someone does something you don't like, doesn't mean you should light off on them, demanding they stop this or shouting,"You're not going to do that to me."

What it does mean is that we speak up, respectfully, calmly and firmly, engaging a discussion about what just occurred or what was said. When you have a complainer in your ear, you smile and say, "I can appreciate your situation. Right now, I'm working on this project which is due at noon. Maybe you should you take this up with your supervisor." Then go about your work. You are proclaiming the message that this is not the time, and you are the not the one who listens to complainers without solutions.

When your manager comes in with his new priorities for your day, smile and convey the choices you both have and the consequences of those choices. "I'm glad you are confident in my abilities to get this done. Right now, I'm working on this report which is due at the two o'clock staff meeting. If I do this new project, the report won't get done; in fact, it'll be pushed off until next week. Would you like me to finish this report and then start on your project, or push the report to next week and do the new project now?"

You are communicating your schedule and the consequences of choices. More importantly, you are teaching that you can't be dumped on anytime anyone wishes. What we allow -- We teach.

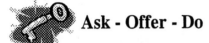 ## Ask - Offer - Do

Ask - Offer - Do. Rallying individuals into a common cause is not easy, and, not that difficult, as well. Where most leaders fail is by telling or demanding rather than asking and offering. They may ask your opinion but, then, do it their way, in spite of your suggestions, only reinforcing the true agenda which was: their way or the highway. Talking, telling and doing something else does not inspire but, rather, alienates. Demanding does not draw people together but, rather, sets individuals apart.

An alternative to telling and demanding is to apply a system found in *Getting it Done: how to lead when you're not in charge.* The author says we should *ask* someone to contribute his thoughts, while explaining the purpose of our question (so as not to imply a secret agenda), then *offer* your own thoughts while inviting others to challenge your thinking, then *do* something constructive. This system goes a long way in creating strong allegiance and loyalty. It allows everyone to have a say and know they are valued for their perspective and insights.

The Window and the Mirror

Successful leaders look out the *window* to apportion credit to factors outside themselves when things go well (and, if they cannot find a specific person or event to give credit, they credit good luck). At the same time, they look in the *mirror* to apportion responsibility, never blaming bad luck when things go poorly. The opposite is a person who looks out the window for something or someone outside himself to blame for poor results, but will preen in front of the mirror and credit himself when things went well. Strangely, the window and the mirror do not reflect objective reality.

Everyone outside the window points inside saying, "Without his guidance and leadership, we would not have been so successful." And the true leader points right back out the window and says, "Look at all the great people and great fortune that made this possible; I'm a lucky guy."

They're both right.

Effective Teaching Techniques

Transference of values and principles doesn't just happen. It occurs through teaching. Teaching takes forethought and planning rather than flying by the seat of your pants. I consider every meeting an opportunity to teach. I can teach a value, an objective, a manner of how we will go about accomplishing something. Sometimes I'm teaching through my own actions and responses to circumstances. No matter the method, every contact, every conversation we have with another individual, is an opportunity to teach.

Follow these guidelines, and you will be more effective in teaching. Once you understand the proper way to transfer information and skill sets, then never stop teaching. Don't ever stop. There is no final destination for this; there is only the journey in a quest for a successful revolution.

I've been asked many, many times, "When did you leave your radio career and begin teaching?"

My answer is, "I've always been in the business of teaching. It didn't matter whether it was in the broadcasting field, as a grocery warehouse supervisor, a sales manager or pastor. It has always been a required element of my leadership to continuously be teaching."

And so it should be for you.

Here, then, are the questions that must be answered in order to effectively teach.

What are the training objectives?

What will be included in your training program elements?

Where does learning occur?

What method of training will be used?

How will you decide if the training is any good?

What are your training objectives? This is the most important stage of training: planning your instructional objectives. Review Step 2: Establish Your Goal, and you'll see again the importance to, as Steven Covey would say, "begin with the end in mind." There are three characteristics of a training objective:

> **It's specific -- not general, broad or fuzzy.**
> **It's measurable, observable and tangible.**
> **It will describe the participant's performance -- the**
>   **desired outcome.**

State your training objective using action verbs and the context in which the behavior occurs -- such as: "The trainee will identify the blue bags and place them in a cardboard box until full." Or, "The employee will demonstrate a positive attitude by smiling, greeting people and thanking them for their assistance."

Break down every training session into specific instructional objectives, and you will be able to better follow through on the remaining required questions.

 What will be included in your training elements? Effective teaching will include the following in each session:

Pre-training assessment built around your instructional objectives
• This can be a short quiz in verbal or written form. The object is to demonstrate what someone *doesn't* know. Without a need, there is little motivation for learning.

Presentation of information and materials
• Use the five senses. Send the information through different filtering processes in the brain -- the more filters, the better the information is retained.

Participant exercises demonstrating achievement of objectives
• The participant performs the new skill, either individually or within a group.

Discussion of participant exercises
- Participants and instructor, together, critique the performance, offering alternative techniques or expanding the thought process in order to make a better decision.

Review of learned material
- Repeat the instructional objective and the path to its successful completion.

Post-training assessment with differently-loaded items
- Alter the wording or style of questions in order to assess the actual retention and application of the information presented and practiced.

Participation evaluation
- How was the learning process? Did they feel it will contribute to their success?

Where does learning occur? The following chart illustrates where the adult learning process is most productive. All steps are important, but only as building blocks to the end result.

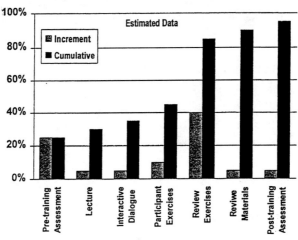

Notice that the cumulative learning bar dramatically rises during the review of exercises, review of materials and post-training assessments. This is where the collective knowledge is shared and exchanged.

We assume incorrectly that learning takes place with our lecture, our homework, our dialog and notes. So we prepare them to be well-organized, understandable, logical and entertaining. Although these may be helpful, they are not the birthplace of real learning.

If you rely on exams as a measurement of success, participants can just guess and get 25% correct. A clearly-delivered multi-media presentation achieves little, and repetitions of a single message are generally going to be less than 17 (the magic number of repetitions to "get it"). Therefore, 100% learning is rare. It is in the review of participant exercises, review of the materials, and in the post-training assessment that you will achieve the success you are looking for.

What method of training will be used? The Socratic method of presentation is an effective and collaborative style of training. The Socratic process has the following characteristics:

> Ask, don't tell
> Give clues to answers
> Ask respondents for more detail, amplification
> Ask for disagreement
> Ask for definition of the opposite
> List participant answers
> Compare participant answers with the clues

The exercises can be individual or in groups. They need to have clear instructions that are explained aloud, using different words for complete understanding. If they are to work in groups, more than six to a group will require the assignment of a leader. Less than six and a natural leader will emerge. Assign different problems to different groups or people. Circulate among the groups offering assistance when stuck.

When reviewing the exercises, have the participants describe their answers while encouraging the others to add, enhance or append with corrective input. Solicit minority opinions while referring back to the written material. Facilitate a consensus to the exercise.

Always review what you have covered at the resumption after a break, at the beginning of a new day, and at the end of that day's session. Ask participants to identify key skills to achieve the objective. Respond verbally and ask the group for any corrections.

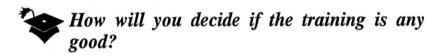 *How will you decide if the training is any good?*

Which of the following would you choose as a valid means to determine if the training was effective to your overall objectives?

- ☐ Participants received information in class

- ☐ Participants are satisfied with the training

- ☐ Participants learned something

- ☐ Participants pass an examination

- ☐ Participants demonstrate ability to behave in new ways they could not before

- ☐ Participants have improved insight into subject matter

❑ Participants are able to retain information two weeks after training

❑ Participants change day-to-day behavior

The answer is the continuum. If you read the list from top to bottom and consider it a low to high scale of learning, then the answer is: if all they received from the class was information -- the training was a failure. Whereas, if your student was able to change his daily behavior to reflect the desired outcome -- then you have succeeded. You can use this list to gauge exactly how far you progressed in any specific session and use future training opportunities to reach an even higher level.

A simplified sequence of the learning process would be:

>>   Explain the Why
>>   Show the How
>>   Let them Practice
>>   Review and Reflect

Revolutionary Tactics to Pass the Baton

➡ Use the leadership quick keys on a daily basis. Make them YOUR techniques to open doors of cooperation and particiation:
Say "Yes . . . and"
Ask "What if . . ."
Ask "What would it take to . . ."
What we allow – we teach
Ask – Offer – Do

➡ Apply the formula for more effective teaching time. Ask:
What are the training objectives?
What will be included in your training program elements?
Where does learning occur?
What method of training will be used?
How will you decide if the training is any good?

➡ Follow the sequence for learning:
Explain the Why
Show the How
Let them Practice
Review and Reflect

STEP 8	Celebrate and Unite
STEP 7	Pass the Baton
STEP 6	Stay Focused and Organized
STEP 5	Increase Commitment
STEP 4	Manage The Change
STEP 3	Build A Coalition
STEP 2	Establish Your Goal
STEP 1	Set Your Foundation

Step 8: Celebrate and Unite

*"Happiness is this moment . . .
for this moment is your life."*

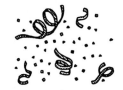

Phil Jackson, legendary coach of the six time champion Chicago Bulls and three time champion (as of this writing) Los Angels Lakers, was once asked during an interview, "How do you get millionaire babies to play together?"

Good question. How DO you get a group of individuals such as these to cooperate and coordinate their efforts in unison, one of whom is 19 years old with 90 million bucks in his pocket without yet sinking a single basket in his professional career? Why should they cooperate? What could possibly motivate them?

This question is no different than the one we have to ask ourselves if our revolution is to fully succeed regarding individuals with whom we work. Our people may not have soft drink and sneaker endorsement deals, but they are human beings with the same hopes and dreams for a "championship" season, however that is defined.

Phil's response took him back to a time when a young kid from North Carolina came to the Bulls with his own dreams of a championship. Phil took this fledgling kid named Michael into his office said, "You will never win an NBA championship."

What? What kind of motivation is that? You're suppose to tell him what a great asset he will be to the team. You're suppose to tell him his dreams will come true if he applies himself, works hard and dedicates all his energy to this one goal. You're suppose to pat him on the back and declare your support for this phenomenal, young talent. Tell him he will never win an NBA championship?

"You will never win an NBA championship . . .
until you raise the playing level of your teammates."

Phil said the same thing coming to L.A., taking aside the likes of Shaquille O'Neil, who seemed to possess the strength and power of Superman (as demonstrated by the emblem tattooed on his arm), yet, struggled, never attaining the ultimate prize.

"You will never win an NBA championship . . .
until you raise the playing level of your teammates."

Did Michael Jordan or Shaquille O'Neil ever win an NBA championship by themselves? Could they? Of course not. With all their talent and innate God-given abilities, they alone, could not and would not ever win a championship. They had to raise the level of success with each of their teammates. Not make them play like Mike or Shaq, but, rather, raise THEIR individual playing levels to new heights.

To accomplish this, Phil had to impart one more insight that would set the course of record-breaking NBA Championships to follow. He concluded his response to the reporter's question with:

"Every human being aspires to something greater than themselves."

This is the key.

We each aspire to something we could never fulfill within ourselves. To view our potential accomplishments by looking at our individual weaknesses and limitations would be like looking at the potential of a race car driver and saying, "He'll never win a race with bad teeth like that."

If Michael Jordan had to play one-on-five every game, just him against the world, it wouldn't take long for even Mike to say, "I can't run fast enough. I can't cover all five opponents at once. I can't score enough points. This isn't for me."

Only by viewing our potential triumphs through the COMBINED efforts of all individuals contributing their talents, sweat and ideas, can we begin to aspire to do what we could never do alone. When it comes to leading the people of your revolution, the sand trap that continues to hinder your team's potential is the misunderstood difference between rewards and motivations.

Rewards vs. Motivation

One reason our revolution has not worked in the past is that we have confused rewards with motivation. It's an easy thing to do, since rewards seem to drive the effort at getting specific things done.

A sales goal was met when tied to a cash bonus.

Overtime was agreed upon in exchange for additional time off.

Tasks were completed early when an offer of pizza & ice cream was extended.

Even at the tender age of six, my dad offered the reward of a sundae if I said my lines correctly during a Sunday School production. The problem was, I didn't know that a "sundae" meant ice cream. I thought my dad meant I'd get "Sunday" off from going to church! It still worked -- I said my lines on cue (and I was still happy with our stop at a local drive-in for my reward afterwards).

Rewards do get certain things done, usually for a short and specific period of time. The problem is, after the reward window is closed, we may or may not achieve the same results again.

Which is why I stopped giving cash as a reward. It wasn't that the extra $20 or $50 or $100 went unappreciated by the person who received it. The issue, I discovered, was that, after the money was spent, after the gas tank was filled, the groceries purchased or dinner eaten, would anyone remember how they earned the money?

No. It was gone. Consumed. Almost as if it had never existed. After all, we will have to eat again, and the gas tank will run dry. There wasn't a single memory to guide and assist them in accomplishing the same result in the future.

Rewards work, but they don't last.

Motivation is different.

Motivation is what gets us out of bed.

Motivation is deeper and not tied to external, temporary compensation. Motivation is what moves people to do things they wouldn't normally do, achieve things they could never conceive of achieving themselves.

Motivation IS tied directly to personal value. The more you can tap into his intimate sense of undeniable worth as a created human being, the more apt he will follow you to the ends of the earth. In a deranged manner, the cultivating of this individual self-worth is at the heart of most cults. The cult has provided an environment to supplant the personal value that an individual would normally find in his traditional family or community setting, with its own perverse sense of significance.

As humans, no matter how independent we may claim to be, we each need to feel we have merit in this life, that we have something to contribute to a greater good, a higher cause.

That's when I decided that if I was going to motivate people, if I was going to create long-lasting impact, then I needed something more. That's when we created P.E.M.

P.E.M.
Positive Emotional Memories

I believe that PEM can motivate people today and far into the future. PEM goes beyond the moment and is ingrained in the recipient's brain forever. PEM becomes folklore and tales that grow in depth and breadth with each recitation over time. PEM becomes a culture, a way of doing things, a way we treat each other. Here is an example of PEM.

A client in Houston provides the raw drugs that pharmacies use to mix and concoct a wide range of medications. These raw drugs are ordered primarily over the internet. After I had taught the principles of PEM in a previous workshop, I had returned for a follow-up seminar six months later. In the middle of my workshop, mid afternoon sometime, the intercom blasted into the conference room where I was training and demanded, "Everyone come to the cafeteria for a special announcement. RIGHT NOW!"

Immediately, everyone got up from their chairs and walked out of the room, leaving me standing there wondering what to do. Fire drill? Free food? What was there to do except follow?

Over 200 employees had packed themselves, shoulder-to-shoulder, in the normal habitat of lunch meat, corn chips and Coca-cola, standing in suits, gowns or whatever work clothes were appropriate to their positions. The CEO walked to the front, making his way through the maze of crowded space. I strained on tip-toe to see over all the heads. Without introduction, he barked out, "Does everyone remember what happened to us last Friday?"

A groan went through the crowd. Someone whispered from behind, explaining the disaster. All their computers had crashed. No internet. No orders. No business.

He continued. "What you don't know is that three people spent the next 72 hours, over the weekend, making sure we were up and running again by Monday. I want you to know who they are." And he announced the names of three people, motioning them to come forward. These were ordinary, I.T. (Information Technology) type people, uncomfortable being in front of large crowds (which is more than two people from their point of view), preferring to work alone amidst their capacitors, patch cords and key boards. The three stood awkwardly, hands behind their backs, swaying from one foot to the other, a bit embarrassed by the whole thing.

The CEO turned and opened a medium-sized, wooden, rectangular box. He took out a CD, just a plain, normal CD that any of us would use, but these had something written across the top and bottom (I couldn't see what it said from the back of the room; I assumed it would approximate "Congratulations" or something similar). Running through the hole in the middle was a red, white and blue ribbon. The CEO walked over to each of the three honorees and, placing the CD medal "award" around their neck, he said, "For going above and beyond the call of duty, we honor you today."

An Olympic ceremony couldn't have been more meaningful. And you should have seen how much straighter and taller those three were standing with the medal around their neck. They were proud and happy, grinning sheepishly to each other.

A cake was rolled out that had their names inscribed with icing. The CEO concluded with, "Everyone shake the hand of these three, grab a piece of cake, and get back to work."

The whole event took maybe 20 minutes.

My question is, what would have been remembered more: an extra $100 in their paycheck or a cheesy, homemade "medal" that will hang next to their computer for the rest of their lives?

That's PEM. The story will live on forever and inspire others in that company to do together what they couldn't do themselves. After seeing the enormous benefits of PEM, why don't we use this instrument of motivation more often?

Because it's easier to write a check.

PEM dictates a bit more time to think about what to do, taking a little more effort. But the affects and outcomes last so much longer and are so much more motivating. And in the end, PEM will always be more cost effective than handing out money. You could pass out $50 bills to every individual within your company or department, or, for less money, you could design a PEM that will last a lifetime.

Tips to Create a Long-lasting PEM

Take lots of pictures. Make sure the honored person(s), and everyone involved with a specific project or success, gets a framed copy. Don't make it big or gaudy. A simple 3x5 plastic holder works just fine. It's the picture that triggers the PEM.

Vary the modes of memorialization. Use handwritten notes, a symbolic award, a certificate, a medal, a trophy, anything that is permanent and will survive as long as the person receiving it. If you choose to use flowers, always include a note or card for the person to keep after the plant has gone to vegetation heaven.

Personalize it. Use the person's name. Be specific about what he or his team accomplished. Customize the memory to individual tastes and preferences.

Don't ever do business during the PEM event. Set this aside as a time all unto itself. The normal business of the day needs to be suspended. Don't make any announcements not directly tied to the PEM. This is THEIR moment. Keep it pure.

Create a public display. Make an official public version of the picture or award that can be exhibited in the lobby or public viewing area. Let the outside world know you are proud of them. Let customers see your PEM culture at work. The tribute doesn't have to stay there forever. Only until the next PEM event.

Understanding the difference between rewards and motivation will be the difference between haltingly, sporadic advances or long-lasting, satisfying successes. Use rewards sparingly for a specific period of time, while continuously planning your next PEM opportunity to motivate.

The Secret Word for Success

I discovered the secret word for motivational success in a Cajun cookbook, not the normal place one would think to look for the key to celebrating and uniting a revolution. Yet, there it was. It's a word rarely used outside Louisiana. New Orleans has two restaurants and a newspaper by the same name. The secret word for a successful culminating effort to create loyalty and admiration with your team, co-workers, your board of directors, your family, customers, both internal and external is . .

Lagniappe

Lagniappe is defined as: a little something extra, a little something more AFTER the recipe is done. This is a very important distinction. Lagniappe is most effective and memorable AFTER the core product or service has been delivered. It's what comes LAST.

In cooking terms, lagniappe is the spice your grandma throws into the pot after she's done making the stew, that little extra kick, that little added umph that would make you say, "Ooooo, that is so good." She'd say it was just something she threw together. We now know it as the lagniappe.

Lagniappe is not directly connected to leadership activities, the service or core product itself. It is not a substitution for quality work. In fact, lagniappe assumes that you will produce a quality product, you will perform excellent service, you will be an exemplary leader.

That is what is expected as a standard. That is a given as a normal course of your daily endeavors.

Lagniappe, by its definition, is what happens AFTER the quality work is done. It's what a doctor would do AFTER the appointment is completed. It's what a teacher would do AFTER class is released. It's what the shipping department would do AFTER a package is sent on its way. It's what a CEO would offer AFTER a supervisor has completed her work.

Lagniappe, to a customer, is not connected to how large or small they may be. For employees, it's not tied to 30 years of service or surviving as a first week rookie. Lagniappe says, "I expect you be who you should be and do what you should do. I'm the extra bonus after all is said and done."

Lagniappe is what your customer will remember long after the bill has been paid.

Lagniappe is what your co-workers will remember after the project is complete.

Lagniappe is what your employees will remember after they've cashed their payroll checks.

Lagniappe is what your children will remember after they have started a family of their own.

Lagniappe is what your spouse will remember when telling family tales.

Lagniappe is what we remember, the end.

Not the event, the product, not the project, not the service, but the experience of each. It's the experience that we remember. The Mall of America in Minneapolis is not one the country's top tourists attractions because of the shopping -- it's the experience. The American Girl Place in Chicago is not remembered because you can buy a doll there -- it's the experience. Your first airplane ride is not remembered because it got your from point A to point B -- it's the experience.

> *"Anticipation and Remembering are the stuff of life. The event itself goes by so fast, it's almost negligible."*

To pull off a really good lagniappe, follow these three guidelines. All three do not have to be concurrent, but include as many of the three with each lagniappe as possible.

It's random and unexpected. If you give something special to everyone, all the time, it will then be expected by everyone, all the time. If you carry out the packages for every customer, that would be considered "good customer service." It would not be lagniappe. I'm not saying don't give great customer service. What I am saying is, if you want it to be lagniappe, then do something random and unexpected.

For example, in order to encourage customers to eat out on Mondays and Tuesdays, most restaurants offer a discount EVERY week to EVERYONE who comes in. One owner decided to perform lagniappe. Once a month, on any given Monday or Tuesday, he will observe a table where the patrons seem to be having an especially good time. When the bill is delivered, the customer will open it to unexpectedly find a letter. The letter simply says, "Welcome to my restaurant. I saw that you were having an especially good time, and I would hate to inconvenience your evening with a bill. Your dinners tonight are on me." Signed the owner's name.

Think about it. When was the last time you received a FREE meal? Only after you've had a lousy experience...they want to give you another! Here is an example of an owner who is on top of lagniappe. He is going to give a free meal in order to make it an even more memorable experience.

When do you think his busy days of the week are?

You're right -- Mondays and Tuesdays.

It goes above and beyond the norm. Lagniappe is special simply because it's not ordinary. The recipient recognizes that he just received something extra, something that is not a part of the everyday course of business. When warm cookies were first handed out on Midwest Express  Airlines, that was lagniappe. When a hotel called your room five minutes after arriving to check that everything was as expected, that was lagniappe. When a waitress asked where you were from, how your vacation was going, suggested some local sights to take in, that was lagniappe.

Lagniappe goes above and beyond the everyday norm of expected service. Hertz #1 Gold Club took the exasperating experience of renting a car and infused it with lagniappe. Normally, after you get your bags and find the rental car counter, you stand in line, get your car assignment, go find the shuttle bus, ride four miles off lot, get dropped of at another building where you go in, stand in line, hand in your paperwork, get the keys to your car, and are instructed to walk out the doors, turn to your left, go to row Q and car number 13. It'll be somewhere past the palm tree.

With Hertz #1 Gold Club, you get on the shuttle bus, and give the driver your Hertz #1 Gold Club number. While driving to the lot, the driver will enter your number into the mobile computer which will display your assigned car location. He will drive up to the rear of your car, open the bus door, hand you a receipt with "have a nice day," your trunk will be open, the air conditioning or heater turned on (depending on season), and off you go.

Lagniappe goes above and beyond norm.

It invites a person to play. So many people
live hum-drum lives. Everyday is the same: get up,
get the kids off to school, go to work, open the mail,
come home, prepare dinner, do laundry, go to bed,
and so forth and so on. Anytime you can invite
someone to play, you will have created lagniappe.

One commercial printer in Minneapolis, twice a year, cleans out the back press room, prepares a full buffet table, hires a live band to play from 5 p.m.-9 p.m., and invites all his customers, employees and their families to enjoy an evening on him. That's more fun than mailing out a 10% discount coupon on your next printing order.

When our radio station attained the rights to broadcast the baseball games of our local AAA farm team, we didn't just announce it on the air. I bought a 100-pound sack of in-the-shell peanuts, got the team to donate a couple hundred miniature helmets, and every customer we saw for the next month was presented with a mini-helmet filled with peanuts proclaiming, "The Beloit Snappers are on WGEZ." What do you think happened as soon as the helmet was placed on the counter? They couldn't help but begin to eat the peanuts! That's a whole lot more fun than listening some bland, hyped ad on the radio.

Be creative. Have fun with it. The people we are in contact with will remember the playful times, because there seem to be fewer and fewer opportunities for this innocent type of expression.

And it goes without saying, if you should have a complaint or grievance -- lagniappe 'em to death! Knock their socks off with the unexpected, the over-the-top, the fun. In retail business, studies have shown that if you can resolve a complaint to the customer's satisfaction, 70% will become your most loyal customers. And a recent Harvard study showed that if you can **shorten** the time between the complaint and its resolution, over 90% will become your most loyal customers!

Revolutionary Tactics to Celebrate and Unite

➡ Distinguish between rewards and motivation. Rewards are short-term compensation to attain a specific result. Motivation is what gets them out of bed.

➡ Use PEM to motivate: Positive Emotional Memories

➡ Take lots of pictures, vary the modes of memorialization, personalize the event, and don't do any business during the PEM ceremony. Keep it pure.

➡ Create a public display for your PEM honoree. Show off those people and success stories that make everyone proud.

➡ Build Lagniappe into your revolutionary success. Make sure:
   It's random and unexpected.
   It goes above and beyond the norm.
   It invites a person to play.

➡ Use Lagniappe when resolving complaints or grievances. Lagniappe 'em to death.

SUMMARY

"Time refused to be bottled up like a genie stuffed in a lamp. Whether it flows as sand or turns on wheels within wheels, time escapes irretrievably, while we watch. Even when the bulbs of the hourglass shatter, when darkness withholds the shadow from the sundial, when the mainspring winds down so far that the clock hands hold still as death, time itself keeps on.

The most we can hope a watch to do is mark that progress. And since time sets its own tempo, like a heartbeat or an ebb tide, timepieces don't really keep time. They just keep up with it, if they're able."

Every class I teach, whether for entrepreneurs who seek dream of running their own businesses or young students at a technical college just hoping to get a passing grade, every seminar and workshop I facilitate, whether on the topic of customer focus or effective skills for new managers, every conference I keynote, whether for doctors on the topic of patient care or for Crime Stoppers on how to increase public awareness and visibility, every hallway discussion with a band of hopeful, yet skeptical, employees, every conversation I have with my children, I have only one vision I yearn to convey:

You can make a difference in this world.

No matter your position, role or lot in life, rich or poor, healthy or in anguish, swift or slow, encompassed by friends and family or all alone -- you can make a difference in this world. A bumper sticker in Maine reads:

Those who don't support your dreams have given up on theirs.

We are not in need of more money, time or strength. We have what God has given and that is sufficient to create a miracle. Yet, we wait. We wait until our education is finished. We wait until the kids are grown and out of the house. We wait until the chemotherapy is completed. We wait until we feel like it. We wait until our boat comes in, our ship is ashore, our treasure has landed. We wait for our lucky break. We wait until given permission. We wait for our next promotion. We wait until the moon and stars are aligned. We wait and wait and wait.

My friend, the time for waiting is over. This is your revolution. Forever the dream is in the mind -- realization is in the hand. My wish, my goal, my utmost desire is for your mind to perceive and your heart to believe -- you can make a difference in this world.

I wish you enough sun to keep your attitude bright.
I wish you enough rain to appreciate the sun more.
I wish you happiness to keep your spirit alive.
I wish you enough pain so the smallest joys in life appear much bigger.
I wish you enough gain to satisfy your wanting.
I wish you enough loss to appreciate all that you possess.
I wish you enough hellos to get you through the final goodbye.

Start a revolution.

Today.

Analytic Outline

Introduction: You can start a revolution 1

Step 1: Set Your Foundation 15

    Prepare Your Values 18
    Prepare Your Strengths 19
    Prepare Your Weaknesses 21
    Prepare Your Modeling Behaviors 22
    Prepare To Accept Input From Others 24
    Prepare Your Game Plan 27
    Prepare Your Blueprint For Personal Renewal 29

Step 2: Establish Your Goal 33

    4 Principles to Understand about Goals 36
       Great goals attract great people
       Great goals precede resources
       Focusing on great goals opens up resources
       Stop your great goals and resources dry up

    S.M.A.R.T. Goals succeed 38
       Specific
       Measurable
       Action-orientated
       Realistic
       Timely

Conduct Dream Sessions to Expand Your Vision 39
    Choose the proper location
    Everyone affected by the dream must attend
    Follow the Rule:
        Any dream idea cannot be hampered for lack of
        Money, Time or People
    Prioritize the Ideas
        Identify one idea to be completed in the next year
        Identify the objectives needed to complete the idea
        Identify the tasks needed to meet each objective

    Within days, publicly demonstrate work on the first idea

Step 3: Build A Coalition 45

    Choose one other person to share your thoughts 47

    Elicit input from each individual 48
        CBD: Consult Before Deciding
        Ask Questions rather than making statements
        Incorporate their ideas
        Require involvement and contribution

    Consistently schedule times to exchange information . 52
        Purpose: Goals for the meeting
        Thinking: moving logically from symptoms to
          diagnosis to planning
        Learning: preparing, acting, and reviewing
        Engagement: every task has someone responsible
        Feedback: offer appreciation and coaching
          for improvement

    Create Peer Pressure 53
        You must follow-up first
        Be specific
        Take three-four others as witnesses
        Take your idea to a team or management meeting

Create a Mantra 56
    Ten words or less
    Must be doable by everyone
    Must move through time
    Each individual write 2 - 3 sentence ideal
    Circle the theme words of each sentence
    List and link the common theme words
    Keep reducing the word group to ten words or less
    Test your mantra to real-life scenarios
    Communicate your mantra to everyone

Step 4: Manage The Change 71

Recognize the three sources of frustration 73
    Expectations that are not fulfilled
    An intention is blocked
    Feelings are not communicated

You have two choices to managing change 74
    Command and Control
    River Method

Continuously SCAN 77
    Specific information
    Concerns are addressed
    Attitudes are anticipated
    Needs are met for success

WIIFM: What's In It For Me? 79
    Attend to the needs of others first
    Don't make today's circumstances tomorrow's
      sacred cows
    Keep listening and communicating
    Get a new perspective
    Surround yourself and utilize champions
    Build skills of self-observation and correction

Step 5: Increase Commitment 83

  Apply the five stages of the Commitment Cycle 85
      Unaware
      Aware
      Comprehend
      Conviction
      Action

  Two types of people 88
      Laggards
      Innovators

  Move both laggards and innovators 91
      Affiliation
      Acknowledgment
      Authority

  *Use repetition to move people through the
  Commitment Cycle* 95
      Present new information
      Vary the modes of communication

  How to get anyone to do anything 98
      Limit their options
      Work from a deadline
      Vocalize your expectations
      Help them process the information
      Ask the final, critical question

Step 6: Stay Focused and Organized 107

  When facing storms of resistance 109
      Do not run away
      Make small adjustments
      At its worse, move to safe surroundings

Resolve conflict with the Five Rules to Resolution ... 112
   Identify the common objective
   Identify what's missing for a smooth operation
   Identify the physical actions steps
   Identify the benefits for both parties
   Identify the accountability system to adjust and adapt

Common areas in which conflict is found
   The process
   The communication
   The priorities

When dealing with discord up and down the line 117
   Go back one department and apply the five
   rules to resolution
      If peer-to-peer, you may go alone
      If speaking to a manager, have 2-3
      others as witnesses

Avoid the three most common time traps 118
   Procrastination: apply "Take 15"
   Perfectionism: train yourself to let it go
   Carelessness: always set priorities
      Do your "A" level activities first

Follow two tips for a more effective "to do" list 124
   Read your list out loud
   Begin to live Inside/Out to manage interruptions

Step 7: Pass The Baton 133

Apply the leadership quick keys 136
   Say "yes . . . and"
   Ask "what if . . .?"

Ask "what would it take to . . .?"
What we allow - We teach
Ask - Offer - Do

Techniques for more effective teaching 140
What are the training objectives?
What will be included in your program elements?
Where does learning occur?
What method of training will be used?
How will you decide if the training is any good?

The sequence for learning 146
Explain the Why
Show the How
Let them Practice
Review and Reflect

Step 8: Celebrate and Unite 149

Rewards vs. Motivation 151

Apply P.E.M. to motivate 153
Take pictures
Vary the modes of memorialization
Personalize it
Don't do business during PEM
Create a public display

The secret word for success: Lagniappe 157
It's random and unexpected
It goes above and beyond the norm
It invites a person to play

Use lagniappe when resolving complaints or grievances

Summary 165

Lost At Sea Answer and Rationale

According to experts, the basic supplies needed when a person is stranded in mid ocean are articles to attract attention and articles to aid survival until rescuers arrive. Articles of navigation are of little importance. Even if a small life raft were capable of reaching land, it would be impossible to store enough food and water to subsist during the period of time.

Furthermore, most rescues occur during the first thirty-six hours, and one can survive without substantial food and water during this period.

1. **Shaving Mirror:** critical for signaling air-sea rescue.

2. Two-gallon can of oil-gas mixture: the oil-gas will float on the water and could be ignited for a signal (obviously outside the raft!)

3. Five-gallon can of water: necessary to replenish loss by perspiring, etc.

4. One case of U.S. Army C rations: provides basic food intake.

5. **Twenty square feet of opaque plastic:** utilized to collect rain water, provide shelter from the elements.

6. Two boxes of chocolate bars: a reserve food supply.

7. **Fishing Kit:** ranked lower than candy bars because there is no assurance that you will catch any fish.

8. **Fifteen feet of nylon rope:** may be used to lash equipment together to prevent it from falling overboard.

9. **Floating seat cushion:** if someone fell overboard, it could function as a life preserver.

10. **Shark repellent:** obvious.

11. **One quart of 160-proof rum:** used as antiseptic for any injuries, of little value otherwise; will cause dehydration if ingested.

12. **Small transistor radio:** of little value since there is no transmitter (and you are out of range of your favorite AM radio station.)

13. **Maps of the Pacific Ocean:** worthless without additional navigational equipment - it does not really matter where you are but where the rescuers are.

14. **Mosquito netting:** there are no mosquitoes in the mid-Pacific.

15. **Sextant:** without tables and a chronometer, relatively useless.

Mantra Creation Worksheet

1) Establish what you wish your mantra to address (i.e., overall company image, a department goal, greater cooperation between individuals, more positive work environment, etc.).

2) Each individual write 2-3 sentences describing his idea. How would it look feel, sound? How would people act in this ideal situation? Towards each other? What would be the results if successful?

3) Each individual circle the key word(s) from each sentence that summarizes the theme of that sentence.

4) Every individual read his sentences aloud, slowly. Repeat often, if needed. All other individuals identify the key theme words they hear from the reading of each sentence. Write them on an easel and pad for all to see. The author now adds the key words he discovered and adds them to the list.

5) After all sentences have been read and all key theme words are on the pad, circle and connect the commonly linked words and ideas. Connect with lines and circles between each. Begin to draw out common phrases that incorporate the common key theme words.

6) Write the phrases and words on another, clean pad; keep reducing and sharpening the word grouping to 10 words or less. Test the word grouping against a real life scenario. Does the word grouping give guidance to correct thoughts and actions? If not, keep refining to its absolute core.

7) When satisfied the mantra fulfills its objective, then design a system for communicating it throughout all departments and functions. Create ways to spotlight its existence and application throughout every department.

Notes

STEP 1

P. 6 *Lots of People:* Rudolph Giuliani, *Leadership* (New York: Miramax Books, 2000), p. 70.

P. 12 *The Little Difference:* Bruce Wilkenson, *Prayer of Jabez* (Sisters, OR: Multonomah, 2000), p. 9.

P. 14 *Oh that you would:* I Chronicles 4:9, *The Holy Bible* (Zondersan, 1973 NIV).

P. 16 *Losers live the:* Dennis Waitley, *How to Build Your Child's Self-Esteem* (Nightingale-Conant, 1989), audio cassette.

P. 17 *When a fish swims:* Phil Jackson, *Sacred Hoops* (New York: Hyperion, 1995), p. 34.

P. 21 *Soar with your strengths:* Roger Fisher, *Program of Instruction for Lawyers* Harvard Law School, seminar quote, 2003).

P. 23 *Motor Mimicry:* Malcolm Gladwell, *The Tipping Point* (New York: Little Brown, 2000), p. 84.

P. 23 *Directly modeling behavior:* Roger Fisher, *Getting It Done* (New York: Harper Collins 1998), p. 30.

P. 23 *We normally think:* Ibid, p. 85.

P. 24 *The Armillary Sphere:* Steve Walrath., *Uncommon Sense for Unreasonable Times* (Haverford, PA: Infinity, 2003), pp. 18-22.

P. 29 *People are often:* Wayne W. Dyer, *There is a Spiritual Solution to Every Problem* (New York: Harper Collins, 2001), pp. 106-108.

STEP 2

P. 33 *Direct your life:* Linus Mundy, *Slow Down Therapy* (St. Meinarad, IN, Abby Press, 1990), p. 12.

P. 33 *Your yacht sinks:* Structured Experience Kit, University Associates, San Diego, CA, 1980.

P. 36 *Great Goals:* Adapted from John C. Maxwell, *Developing Partnerships in the Church,* audio cassette.

STEP 3

P. 45 *We have all:* Kenneth Cloke and Joan Goldsmith, *The Art of Waking Up,* Corporate Report Wisconsin, May 2003, p. 6.

P. 45 *Consider the following:* Malcolm Gladwell, *the Tipping Point* (New York: Little Brown, 2000), p. 11.

P. 48 *Always consult before:* Roger Fisher, *Getting It Done* (New York: Harper Collins, 1998), p. 197.

P. 50 Johnny Carson, *Johnny Calls It a Night,* p. 295.

P. 51 *This group mentality:* Malcolm Gladwell, *The Tipping Point* (New York: Little Brown, 2000), pp. 27-28.

P. 52 *People do things:* Lori Veit, *A Cure for Wanderlust,* Corporate Report Wisconsin, May 2003, p. 23.

P. 52 *Purpose, thinking:* Roger Fisher, *Getting It Done* (New York: Harper Collins, 1998), p. 187.

P. 61 *A study was done:* Malcolm Gladwell, *The Tipping Point* (New York: Little Brown, 2000), p. 96.

STEP 4

P. 73 *Expectations that are:* Robert W. Lauridsen, *How to Build Relationships That Work,* High Technology Careers, 1999.

P. 74 *The Chinese character:* Richard N. Bolles, *The Three Boxes of Life* (Berkeley, CA: Ten Speed Press, 1978), p. 31.

P. 75 *Consider the launch:* Diane L. Couter, *Sense and Reliability,* Harvard Business Review, April 2003, p. 86.

P. 76 *A cosmology episode:* Ibid, p. 88.

STEP 5

P. 90 General Wesley K. Clark, quoted in *Esquire,* August 2003, p. 97.

P. 93 *There is a strong:* Diane L. Couter, *Sense and Reliability,* H.B. Review, April 2003, p. 87.

STEP 6

P. 107 *The moment:* C.S. Lewis, as quoted in *Just Like Jesus,* Max Lucado (Nashville: Word Publ., 1998), p. 71.

STEP 7

P. 133 *As you live:* Susan LePage Simmons, *A Friendship Wish,* 1992.

P. 134 *You are building:* Roger Fisher, *Program of Instruction for Lawyers,* Harvard Law School, Seminar 2003.

P. 139 *Ask-offer-do:* Roger Fisher, *Getting It Done* (New York: Harper Collins, 1998), p. 27.

P. 140 *Successful leaders:* Jim Collins, *Good to Great* (New York: Harper Collins, 2001), p. 35.

P. 141 *What are the:* Phillip Blackerby, *Adult Learning Training Methodology,* Manufacturing Systems & Technology, U.S. Dept. of Commerce, 1998.

SUMMARY

P. 165 *Time refused:* Dava Sobel, *Longitude* (Walker and Co., 1995), pp. 34-35.

Workshops available from
The Center For Customer Focus

Keynote Presentations (or ½-day and 1-day workshops)
An inspiring set of topics to motivate and challenge your staff, organization, conference, banquet or seminar.

☆ *Dynamics of Customer Focus* - This is <u>NOT</u> Customer Service! This is an enlightening, energetic, eye-opening presentation in which all individuals in your organization looks at performing their tasks through the eyes of the customer with a view to adding value to the customer's experience.

☆ *Cultivating Winners from Within* – Everyone wants to find the best people to work with. Many times they are sitting right next to us. Learn the secrets to successful People Management which bring diamonds out of the rough and help you recognize and eliminate those who choose not to work within the team system.

☆ *How to Turn Quotes Into Cash* – Sales is wonderful and challenging, but only if the salesperson masters the skills and attitudes necessary to turn a prospective customer into your paying customer. Learn the inside tips to developing effective sales relationships from a 22-year sales veteran who turned a broadcasting business around from a $10,000 monthly loss to over $500,000 in 3 years!

☆ *The Art of Getting Things Done* – We can only be productive with the skills of managing multiple projects, priorities and deadlines. Learn the principles of time and personal resource management to be the most effective manager and employee possible.

☆ *5+5=11 (or more): How to Promote and Market Anything* – The myth of the "used car salesman" is debunked and replaced with the essential elements to make a successful sale and presentation. Learn the principles of why and how we buy including emotion vs. logic and the principle of ownership.

☆ *Supervisory Skills for New Managers* – Employees are only as effective as their managers. This workshop will teach the new supervisor how to successfully coach and lead their staff to greater productivity while creating a team atmosphere. A MUST for all people in their new and challenging position as Manager.

☆ *Using Change as a Catalyst for Growth* – Change is a part of every business – everyday. People, policies, mergers and acquisitions all create change. Your staff and management will learn the principles of successful change that create an atmosphere of trust and move your company forward in a positive and productive manner.

☆ *Overcoming Negativity in Life, Work and Home* – Negativity can creep into anyone's life and work. You will learn the signs of personal, departmental ad organizational negativity and how to deal with each effectively. Create a positive environment with positive people.

☆ *Developing a Successful Personal Path in Work, Family and Life* – Life is made up of decisions and changes. How we act, react and interact will determine our path and its satisfaction to us. Learn how to recognize life's little "tests" and how to pass them with flying colors. Take charge of your life rather than letting life happen to you.

☆ *Dynamics of Customer Focus (2-day)* – Increase you company's competitive advantage by helping managers look at the business through the eyes of the customer. Participates leave empowered with the tools to increase customer focus in their organization and to identify specific customer-focused actions to be implemented.

Customization
Each of our workshops is customized to bring out your industry's current issues as well as your particular struggles. The facilitator will discuss your situation in-depth prior to your workshop.

Steve Walrath

Steve Walrath is a 25-year radio broadcast professional. He has worked in all areas of broadcasting including on-air, news, sales, management and owning/managing his own properties. He took over ownership of a 1000-watt Am radio station and, within 5 years, transformed it into an international corporation of over six divisions, including printing, publishing, broadcasting, catalog center, retail and wholesale travel, computer diagnostics, custom clothing and commercial real estate.

With this success, Steve has taught the principles of Customer Focus, Cultivating Winners from Within, Creating Employee Commitment, Effective Management Skills, and many more topics to such clients as General Motors, Roman Meal Bread Co., Professional Compounding Centers of America, Wisconsin Physicians Service, Trek Bicycles Worldwide, Kansas Medical Society and hundreds more across the United States, Canada and Australia.

Steve earned his Bachelors and Masters Degrees in Business Management, is a certified instructor in Entrepreneurship for FastTrac, an instructor for the University of Wisconsin-Small Business Development Center, and is the founder of the DTS Foundation, Inc., holding seminars to help divorced parents protect and preserve their relationships with their kids.

Steve is the author of *A Divorced Parent's Guide to Seeing Your Kids: What judges, attorneys and your ex have not told you,* and *Uncommon Sense for Unreasonable Times: How to live a life that matters.* Steve also stays active as President for Crime Stoppers International, is the past president of the YMCA, and numerous other not-for-profit organizations.

His keynotes, workshops and seminars have been rated "A+, relevant to the needs of today. The best speaker this conference has ever had and bring him back for more."

More information can be found at his web site: www.stevewalrath.com.